Vasa, The King's Ship

Vasa

The King's Ship

Commander
BENGT OHRELIUS

Translated by Maurice Michael

CHILTON BOOKS

A DIVISION OF CHILTON COMPANY
Publishers
Philadelphia and New York

Contents

Illustrations

A sewing-box contained a comb, thimble, thread and
   some bits of cloth
Beer tankard
Wooden spoon
Brandy keg
Butter keg
Some more household finds

A seventeenth-century seaman who was caught under
   one of the gun-carriages
The remains of another victim of the catastrophe
Another of *Vasa*'s guns was found on 6 June 1961
All the mud and slime inside the ship, which contained
   thousands of interesting objects, was sifted in specially
   constructed sieves
The King of Sweden inspecting one of the journals
   recording finds
The gun-carriages still stand in their places on the lower
   battery-deck
Archæologists at work on the lower battery-deck
Work on the lower battery-deck nearing completion
A part of the seventeenth century
Ten thousand litres a minute spurting out of *Vasa*
The chains being fixed on the hydraulic jacks on the
   pontoon
Vasa lying between the two pontoons, *Oden* and *Frigg*
The last few yards into the safety of the dry dock were
   very critical

Vasa sailing into the dock on her own keel
The big *Vasa* pontoon being docked in Stockholm after
   its voyage from Gävle

LINE-DRAWINGS

(*Unless otherwise stated, line-drawings are by Magnus
  Gerne and Nils Stödberg*)

1. *Vasa, The King's Ship*

The time-machine is a fascinating product of man's imagination, but so far no one has been able to make one. Maybe it is an impossible idea altogether. But curiosity and inquisitiveness are great incentives, so perhaps one day people really will be able to travel through the centuries. Till then, however, we must leave H. G. Wells's idea to the world of science-fiction, to which for the time being it belongs.

Anyway, we do not need a machine to be able to travel through time, backwards at least. What about the tombs of the Pharaohs, the palace of Knossos, and *Vasa*, the seventeenth-century man-of-war recently rediscovered in the waters of Stockholm harbour, where the great ship had been lying in the muddy depths for more than 300 years?

The discovery of *Vasa* has not only stimulated research into the life and manners of the seventeenth century, but has itself contributed considerably to our knowledge of conditions at sea and the art of shipbuilding in those days. It has sent the historians to their archives and already they have unearthed much interesting material, and the brief story of the great ship is now known in most of its details, but the history of its discovery, or rediscovery, is considerably longer and in many ways more exciting than that of the ship itself.

Kindly fate and the efforts of Anders Franzén have

saved this unique man-of-war for posterity. And how easily it might have been destroyed! In recent years enormous quantities of rock have had to be blasted out to make room for the foundations of the new skyscrapers that are changing Stockholm's skyline. This rock has been dumped at various points, building up the banks of Stockholm's waterways. When the big Gustav V dock was being built, quantities of stone and rock were tipped quite near where, unsuspected, *Vasa* was lying. In 1955, the protests of an outraged public saved Riddarfjärden, the waters between the old City and Mälaren, from being turned into a tip for stones and rock, and the city councillors decided, instead, to tip the rock, that would be dug out while building the underground, into those very waters where *Vasa* was. This decision acted as a new incentive to the age-old search for the lost ship, and resulted in her at last being found.

The man behind the discovery, Anders Franzén, is an 'oil-man' by profession and for the last few years chief engineering secretary at the Swedish Admiralty. He is a man who has been curiously lucky in that he has managed to realize every boy's dream of hunting for treasure, which he has done mostly at the bottom of the sea, and with considerable success. Searching for sunken wrecks became a passion with him, a passion that has laid claim to nine-tenths of his spare time. Nowadays, it is seldom, if ever, that one makes money by treasure-hunting, and certainly money is not Franzén's object. In fact, according to Swedish law, every wreck that can be identified belongs to the previous owner or his heirs, if such can be found. The wrecks Franzén searches for have all been men-of-war and as such, quite simply, belong to the State. Thus, far from making money, this hobby of his has proved a rather expensive one, and he has had to put his hand into his own pocket to the tune of thousands of pounds in order to indulge it. What really makes him do all this is a burning interest in marine history. He is most attracted by the men-of-war of the sixteenth and seventeenth centuries, because so little is known of naval architecture and the art of shipbuilding in those days. He is a man, if you will forgive the pun, who likes to get to the bottom of things.

For many years Franzén worked in conjunction with the Museum of Maritime History, locating and investigating wrecks that the museum considered to be of especial interest to it. Some years ago ten or fifteen suitable objects were selected, and of these about half have been located and investigated. It is due to Franzén's work that this museum is the first in the world to have been able to include marine archæology among its ordinary activities, but we Swedes are lucky in living beside a sea that is singularly rich in this respect. The fleets of the great powers have fought many a life-and-death struggle in the waters of the 'peaceful sea', the Baltic. On more than one occasion, big men-of-war have been driven by wind and seas on to shores bristling with shoals and reefs, where they have foundered. Others have gone down in battle, flags flying, defeated by a superior opponent. The Baltic is a happy hunting-ground for those interested in old ships, for its brackish water is most merciful to old timbers and *Teredo navalis*, the shipworm, and other noxious creatures evidently do not like it.

Today, the bed of the seas and oceans is a new, extensive and difficult field of endeavour. He who wants to make discoveries there must work out special methods of his own, get special tools and have endless patience. If your watch has ever slipped off and into the water from

a boat or landing-stage and you have then tried to find it
on a muddy bottom, you will have some idea of what is
entailed in searching for ships that went down 300
years before, in a position about which you have
only the vaguest indications. Searching for sunken ships
is not for treasure-seekers or adventurers who like to
leave things to chance. Modern marine archæology is a
serious science, though one that has had to wait a long
time to come into being. That it is a serious science is in
many ways the result of the advent of the frogman, who
emerged in and after World War II and is now the
marine archæologist's most valuable assistant.

The frogman provides the flexible, and easily transportable means of investigation that was so badly needed.
It is relatively easy to get a frogman into his equipment
and it need never take long before he is in the water.
There is no need for heavy air-pumps or compressed air
equipment to supply him. Where the classic diver in his
heavy diving-suit walked laboriously and clumsily on the
bottom, stirring up mud and ooze, his rope and air-lines
getting entangled in jagged bits of wreck, his colleague
and in many respects his successor, now swims easily like
a fish. In other words, the bed of the sea has become considerably more accessible. The light diver has also made
it possible to systematize submarine archæology.

The marine archæologist, of course, would not get far
if he devoted all his time to underwater work. That
would be worse than looking for a needle in a haystack.
A very considerable amount of the marine archæologist's
effort is devoted to research on land. Naval histories can
provide clues, which have to be followed up with unre-
mitting patience and diligence. Often they have resulted
in nice little pieces of detective work worthy of a Sherlock
Holmes. Dusty tomes in archives can provide valuable

4

information about sinkings and wrecks. With patience and a modicum of luck, combined with the necessary skill, it is often possible to reconstruct the dramatic series of events that led to the loss of a ship several centuries ago. Perhaps a Lord Chancellor sent a long, detailed report to his king in the field, and this has survived. Or private individuals of importance have written about the event to their families or friends, and these letters have been preserved. Perhaps the loss of a warship gave rise to a court of inquiry or a court martial, and the records of the proceedings have been kept. Lawsuits can provide a lot of information, and there is much to be found in old records, accounts and other documents that can complete the picture of what really happened. Sometimes, surprisingly often, in fact, all these varied pieces of information can be fitted together to make a picture complete enough to be accurate.

There are many questions to be answered before work can actually begin at the scene of disaster. The first obvious one is: where does the wreck lie? What happened to her? Will she have been badly damaged? What did she look like? How many guns was she carrying when she sank? . . . The more information that can be elicited, the easier it will be to locate the wreck and plan salvage operations, always a complicated procedure.

It is often difficult, not to say impossible, to discover from these old sources exact information as to a wreck's position, and a trip to the coast nearest the scene will always be rewarding. The searcher may find in the local Press a reference to nets having caught on some mysterious object on the bottom in the vicinity of the supposed site of the wreck, which will show him that he is on the right track. Tales of wrecks frequently figure in local traditions, handed down from father to son, often for centuries, and can provide astoundingly accurate information. Often there is information to be found at the local church, for church records often record valuable facts. Even gravestones have been known to offer information. Old charts can also contain indications of ships lost and the places where ships have gone down.

Many are the ships to which Anders Franzén has given his special attention. With some, like *The Travelling Man* (*Resande Man*), it was the lost ship's romantic name that first attracted him. *The Travelling Man* was a small ship of twenty-two guns which sank during a storm in the late autumn of 1660 somewhere in the neighbourhood of Landsort (an island in the Baltic due south of Stockholm and about forty-three miles from it as the crow flies). She was carrying a precious cargo of gold and silver objects, and was on her way to Poland where she was taking a Swedish soldier and adventurer, Carl Christopher von Schlippenbach. Schlippenbach had succeeded in interesting Charles XI's regents in an alliance with Poland against Russia, and he was off now with many precious gifts in an attempt to arouse John Casimir's interest in the idea. The good ship, *The Travelling Man*, never reached her destination, and Schlippenbach lost his life when she went down. The following summer, *Resande Man*'s guns, anchors, cordage and sails were salvaged. They also managed to get up some chests containing coins; but after that people forgot all about the wreck and its position remains a secret and a mystery.

One day in the summer of 1920, a fisherman from Bedarö fouled his anchor off the little island of Viksten near Landsort. There happened to be a salvage boat with a diver in the vicinity, and the fisherman asked the diver to go down and try to free his anchor. The diver found that the anchor had caught in an old wreck, which was

6

Many ships met their fate in the Baltic. Here are some of them, marked by Anders Franzén on his wreck-chart

later identified as that of the royal vessel *Riksnyckeln* (*Key of the Realm*), which had gone down in 1628 on her way home from Germany with wounded.

We know that in the deep water out in the middle of the channel, between the island of Utö and the inner islands, lies King John III's proud ship *Lybska Ornen* (*The Lübeck Eagle*), which went down in 1576, carrying thirty-three iron guns and twenty-three bronze guns, though we have no idea today what happened or why she

B

was lost. Nor is her exact position known. But there is a sunken rock off Nynäshamn called Orngrundet and this may well have been where *Lybska Ornen* met her fate.

In the days of sail, Dalarö was the port for Stockholm, and the king or his representative often went there to confer with the admirals or to go aboard a ship; yet ships have been lost even in that sheltered harbour. In the summer of 1676, the royal ship *Riksäpplet* (*Apple of the Realm*) was driven on to a small rocky islet by a south-westerly storm and sank in eight and a half fathoms. She had a complement of 500 and carried eighty-six guns. Some of them, which were salvaged, can be seen today at Skansen in Stockholm.

In the same year as *Riksäpplet* was lost at Dalarö, *Gröne Jägaren* (*The Green Hunter*) blew up close to where the other was lost and sank in sixteen fathoms of water.

The admiral's ship of Sweden's first regular fleet, *Lybska Svan* (*The Swan of Lübeck*), which King Gustavus Vasa bought from Germany, has lain since 1525 in Nämdö channel, immediately north of Dalarö, where she sank in twenty-four fathoms of water. She went down carrying a lot of people with her and also a quantity of booty taken from the Danes. It is very probable that the king himself witnessed the catastrophe. This ship had played a considerable part in the War of Independence that, in 1523, finally freed Sweden from Denmark, dissolving the union that had been in existence, off and on, since 1363.

Off Strangnäs lies the so-called *Riksvasa*, which King Sigismund built. The name Brännskeppet on the chart of the area still records the disaster.

In Nybroviken lies a ship of forty-four guns, *Västervik*. She caught fire and sank there in 1676, a disastrous year for Sweden, for it was in June of that year that she was defeated by a combined Danish–Dutch fleet in a big naval engagement off Oland.

But the most sensational find made in the waters of the Baltic is undoubtedly that of *Vasa*. Her discovery was the result of a first-class piece of detective work, the original impetus for which was provided by Professor Ahnlund, for the research which resulted in his identification of *Riksnyckeln* in 1920 also led to the discovery and subsequent publication of a lot of interesting material about her contemporary, *Vasa*. This material included valuable information about the many attempts made to salvage her. Where the disaster actually happened was not clear, however, and no definite information on this point came to light. Nevertheless, this whetted Anders Franzén's appetite and spurred him on to fresh efforts and further research in the old archives. By 1954 he had come to the definite conclusion that she must lie somewhere between Beckholmen and Södermalm. Then for a while he was thrown off the track by the presence of a cross close to Stadsgårdskajen on an eighteenth-century map purporting to mark the position of the wreck. What finally put Franzén on the right track and caused him to shift the scene of his investigation to the correct sector, was the discovery of the report on the castastrophe made by the Council to the king, Gustavus Adolphus II.

The path of the marine archæologist is beset with disappointed hopes, false conclusions and misleading information. Typical of this was the way his attention was diverted from the ship's true position. A detailed chart and map drawn up by Stockholm City Council in connexion with its project for the Osterleden, showed the depths of the water in all this area, most carefully measured by echo-sounder, and recorded the results of sediment samples taken from the bottom and right down to bedrock, which at the deepest point was thirty-five fathoms below the surface. Careful study of this chart revealed a distinct elevation of the bottom just out from the Gustav V dock, where *Vasa* later proved to be lying. The experts whom Franzén consulted about this told him that this hump was made up of rubble and rock blasted out when the Gustav V dock was built, and so he carefully avoided the vicinity of the hump. Then, in 1956, Franzén learned from other quarters that the rock taken out while constructing the Gustav V dock had all been used to fill out the west headland of Beckholmen. But he still did not realize that the hump was *Vasa*.

Although *Vasa* had been lying where she was for 325 years, there was now need to speed up the search, since the city councillors were considering tipping the rock from the building of the Stockholm underground in those very waters, and Anders Franzén accordingly intensified his search.

By the summer of 1956, the following clues had been discovered. The ship was:

1. lying in eighteen fathoms, with correction for elevation of the bottom by sedimentation and man-made means,
2. opposite 'Tegil-wijcken',
3. 'Bleekholmsudden'.

The latter name has never been identified. The museum authorities took it to be identical with Beckholmsodden, which in those distant days had not yet been levelled out; but others have interpreted it as Blockhusudden.

Franzén now took the special map and chart of the area and shaded in all areas south of Beckholmen where the depth was about eighteen fathoms. Everything now pointed to the hump on the bottom outside the Gustav V dock, and when, in August 1956, he managed to fetch up a piece of blackened oak from that spot, he felt that he had enough to justify asking the Admiralty to hold the annual test for naval divers at this spot. This was done and the divers soon discovered *Vasa*'s wreck.

Searching on the bottom in these waters is truly fishing in troubled waters. Over the centuries all sorts of rubbish and refuse from the city have been deposited here, and the marine archæologist who works in Stockholm's waterways is often made to feel like the cartoonist's fisherman who catches an old boot instead of a fish, for his grapnels are continually bringing up old shoes, rusted bicycles and ancient iron bedsteads.

There is considerable boat traffic in this part of Stockholm harbour and that was often a source of serious irritation, while the relatively great depth of the bottom made work difficult. But there were advantages about the position that did much to compensate for such disadvantages. Churches and other prominent buildings made it easy to get bearings for locating suspected 'nibbles'; and also the site was considerably more sheltered from the elements than those Anders Franzén had been accustomed to work in.

Searching the bottom is a long and time-consuming process. It involves sweeping the bed with steel wires, grapnels and touch-sounding. There are many submarine cables in the area and so the grapnels had to be used with extreme circumspection. Each nibble was later investigated individually with a heavy lead on a thin, stainless-steel wire. Any place where there was real suspicion that it might be the one they were looking for was investigated with a special instrument for obtaining samples. This was a sound shaped like an aerial bomb and fitted

11

with stabilizing fins. It is made in such a way that a so-called 'corer' can be fixed to its nose. With this corer it is possible to cut into soft surfaces and obtain round sample specimens of the material, even if it is wood.

2. *The Catastrophe*

Sweden has always been, and still is, largely dependent for her existence on sea transport. The sea has also been her bulwark, and is so now in this atom age as it was in the seventeenth century.

In the early summer of 1628, Wallenstein, that greatest general of the Hapsburg emperors, reached the shores of the Baltic with his troops. The emperor had already appointed him, somewhat previously, 'admiral of the Baltic and oceanic seas', and Wallenstein was preparing to take possession of Stralsund, Wismar and other Baltic seaports, in order to have bases for the fleets that were to make him master of the seas. He even cast greedy looks at the Oresund. With that Baltic highway in his power, he would have been able to control all trade and shipping in the Baltic ports. Such a plan was a grave threat to Sweden's independence.

However, the emperor had no Baltic fleet as yet, though he had decided to send the Spanish fleet to the Baltic in order to reinforce the squadron that Wallenstein had started building at Wismar. If the Spanish ships were to reach the Baltic, the position of the Scandinavian countries would have become precarious indeed. Meanwhile, Stralsund was the aggressive Wallenstein's immediate and most important objective. He intended to make it the headquarters of the imperial fleet. However, that ancient Hanseatic city defended itself heroically against Wallenstein's attack, and he could not take it. In the end, the city was forced to appeal to the northern kings for help, and this was swiftly sent by both the Swedes and Danes, with the result that three months later Wallenstein had suffered such losses that he was forced to withdraw his troops. This was his first setback and a serious blow to his Baltic plans. But he was not the only one with Baltic plans. Sweden now had an important ally in Stralsund and that alliance gave her a footing on German soil. The King of Sweden had his plans, and darker and darker clouds of war gathered over the Baltic.

To carry out his plans the King of Sweden needed men-of-war and impatiently he kept urging his councillors to speed the expansion of the fleet. *Vasa* was an important part of this programme.

In the spring of 1628, the latest addition to the fleet, *Ny Wassan* as she was called originally, was already lying moored near the royal palace of Three Crowns at the so-called gun-crane, and her crew were hard at work getting her ballast aboard and stowing it away. July saw her back by the gun-crane again, this time to take aboard her armament and ammunition from the royal arsenal, which at that time was adjacent to the palace, along with the shot tower and cannon-ball foundry. We are not sure what had been done to her in the meantime, but in all probability she had been warped or towed across to the naval establishment at Gamla Skeppsholmen (now Blasieholmen, where the National Museum is). There, all the other things would have been done to her that could not be done till her ballast was aboard, there being a lot to do before she could be considered properly fitted-out and equipped and ready for the high seas. By 31 July she had all her guns and armament aboard, and the day for her to start out on her maiden voyage was rapidly approaching.

Anders Franzén, *Vasa*'s discoverer

The Vasa arms. Traces of gold were still left on the garb and the crown, while the shield still carries traces of red colouring. Like most of the sculptures, it was found in the mud beside *Vasa*

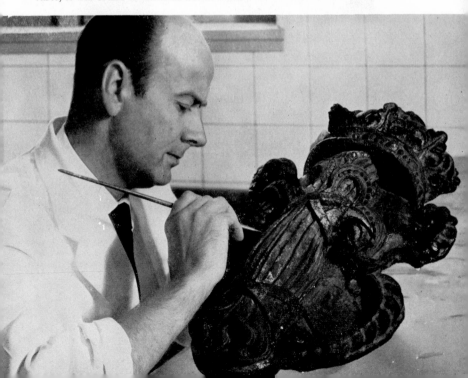

A fine sample of the skill of the seventeenth-century wood-carver, found in the captain's cabin

Details of the Vasa coat-of-arms, which, born by two cherubim, comprised the main decoration of the ship's stern. The house of Vasa reigned in Sweden from 1521—1654

One of the archæologists w
an original sculpture. When t
ship's stern was being dug o
they came across six ang
each with a different musi
instrument. These represen
the heavenly choir, and t
faun being held here eviden
sat underneath, crouching a
clasping his ears in order 1
to hear the music of the sphe

A grimly grinning lion's
face was on the inside of
every gun-port

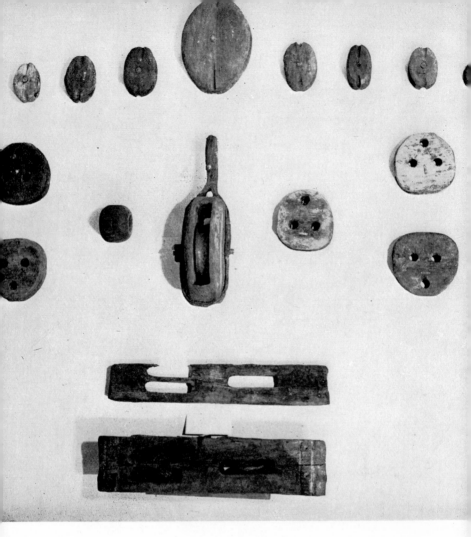

Some details of *Vasa*'s rigging

Earthenware pots for cooking

Wooden vessel

Pewter stoup, probably belong-
ing to one of the officers

Glazed earthenware
bottle

Glazed earthenware plate
with blue ornamentation

Vasa was a big ship, even by international standards. Colourfully painted and lavishly ornamented, she must have made a magnificent picture and called forth considerable comment. The news of her impending departure would have been quickly known throughout the city, and there is no doubt that many people had come down to watch, when, about three or four o'clock in the afternoon of 10 August, her captain, Söfring Hansson, gave the order to cast off.

Slowly *Vasa* was hauled out from her berth at the gun-crane. Her maiden voyage had begun. In still, fine weather she was warped along Skeppsbron, the big, glittering gilded lion that was her figure-head turned towards the heights of Söder, while the men who had been standing ready at the spokes of her big capstan began their tramp round and round, that wound the heavy anchor hawser in. As they trudged, the rhythmic click-click of the ratchets echoed across the water and the heavy hawser came in and coiled on to the deck from the great barrel of the capstan. Meanwhile, one of the ship's boats was already taking out another anchor in readiness for the next warp. Seen on the map now, the distance from the palace to the waters are at the foot of the heights of Söder looks tiny; but when a ship has to cover it relying only on warp-anchors, her capstan and the brawny arms of her crew, it is quite considerable.

Vespers were over and the churches had emptied. Many of the city's 10,000 inhabitants were out enjoying the glories of the lovely summer evening and numbers of them must have decided to go and watch the proud new ship, of which they had heard so much, set out on the start of her maiden voyage. Perhaps, too, they might catch a glimpse of some of the notabilities, who were to accompany her: the master of ordnance, now commanding the fleet to which *Vasa* was to belong, old Captain Jonsson who had been a captain for more than thirty years and had commanded the naval installations at Skeppsholm for many years, and numbers of others. As well as members of the two services, some civilians had also been given leave to sail in the new ship, civilians of both high and low degree, for some of the wives and children of the crew and soldiers she carried were going in her as far as Vaxholm, where they would be put ashore. The service regulations of the time contain the following: 'If anyone wishes to have his wife with him, he is free to do so while his ship is here at Strömmen or in the Skärgarden, but not on a voyage or when proceeding against the enemy.'

Everything on board was lashed down in naval fashion and properly secured; all was ship-shape and ready. All the gun tackles had been pulled taut and belayed, all, that is, except for one small one-pounder, a so-called falcon, which was lying on deck minus its carriage.

West of the oil sheds in Stadsgården (beyond what is now the Saltsjöbaden railway station), they began to prepare to set sail. In order to facilitate the manœuvre of the actual start, Captain Söfring had a cable passed ashore from *Vasa*'s stern, thereby helping her bows to fall off to the east, into the line of her required course. There was now no need for further warping and the anchors were brought in. After this, the people on land could see men entering the rigging and going aloft to unfurl sails. The deck-hands stood ready by the braces, sheets and falls. Then the huge topsails were shaken out on the fore- and mainmasts and stretched, so that they looked like enormous white blinds. Then it was the turn of the foresails, and after that the stern hawser was cast off. *Vasa* had set sail.

Vasa was still in the lee of the high cliffs of Söder and

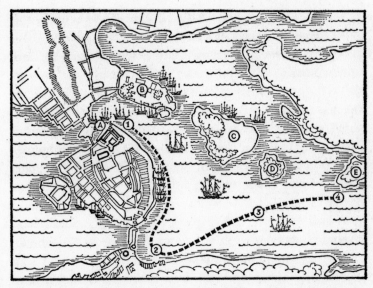

An attempt to reconstruct the route *Vasa* took to disaster on 10 August 1628.

Vasa started from below the royal palace of Three Crowns (1) and was warped against the south-westerly wind to roughly (2), off the oil sheds. At (3) she began to heel over, and (4) marks the place where she sank.

(A) is the oldest shipyard, founded by Gustavus Vasa. (B) is the present Blasieholmen, to which the naval yards were moved at the end of the sixteenth century. (C) is Lustholmen, to which the yards were moved towards the end of the seventeenth century. Its present name is Skeppsholmen. (D) is Kastellholmen. (E) is Beckholmen.

there was only a faint wind to fill her four sails, all that had been set so far, so that the great ship moved only very slowly through the water. She had way on her, but little more. Then the wind increased somewhat, and the water began to ripple round her prow and there must have been a gentle murmuring all along the great hull. She fired the two guns, in those days the conventional signal for departure.

Then a stronger gust off the heights of Söder made the great ship heel over, but she righted herself quite quickly, and glided slowly onwards. The sun was hanging low now, colouring the water and enhancing the richness of the ornamentation on *Vasa*'s after-part. She was still in the lee of the heights, and the many rowing-boats and small craft that were on the water that lovely Sunday evening found no difficulty in keeping pace with her, as they followed in the great ship's wake. From the boats and land people waved to *Vasa*, wishing her and her crew *bon voyage*.

When *Vasa* reached a point opposite where the land curved (the sweep of this has long been straightened off), the wind had more scope and suddenly came as a stiff breeze that made the tall ship heel over strongly and unexpectedly. But again she righted herself. The extent to which she had heeled over was such as to give cause for anxiety, and the captain took his speaking-trumpet and ordered the topsail sheets to be cast loose. Yet already the wind had dropped again and was as soft as before, so faint that it could not even pull the new stiff ropes through the blocks, well greased though they were. As a result they had to be helped through by the deck-hands pushing them.

Then another gust came off the land and again *Vasa* heeled over, farther and farther till water was pouring in through the open gun-ports. Her list became worse and worse, till her rail was touching the water. She was doomed. Immediately off Beckholmen she capsized and went gently to the bottom, flags flying and sail set.

It must have been an incredible sight and many of the good people of Stockholm must have rubbed their eyes and wondered if they had seen aright. Was it possible that such a catastrophe could occur? That one of the

18

king's proudest ships could be lost like that in front of the eyes of the people of the capital? One moment she had been there, proud and lovely, setting out on her maiden voyage, and, suddenly, she was there no longer. Only a few odd objects and planks floating about. And people: men, women and children, some swimming, others struggling desperately and crying out in the fear of death. Thanks to the fact that there were so many boats on the water that evening, helping hands were soon on the spot and all was done to save those who could be saved.

We do not now know how many were aboard *Vasa* when she sailed. According to the documents that have survived, she should have had a crew of 133 and carried 300 soldiers, who acted as gunners, among other duties. To this number must be added the dignitaries aboard and the wives and children of the sailors and soldiers who had elected to sail with her on the first lap of the voyage and who were to be landed at Waxholm, but it would seem now that far fewer people were aboard than was originally thought, for it is fairly certain that the soldiers had not yet embarked when *Vasa* set out on the first stage of her maiden voyage. Nor do we know how many were drowned. It was said that old Captain Hans Jonsson was lost and that Erik Jönsson, the master of ordnance, and *Vasa*'s own captain 'escaped after being under water a long time at great hazard to their lives'. A list of survivors must have been made after the catastrophe, but it has yet to be found. As far as can be judged, it seems likely that some fifty persons lost their lives in the disaster. If she had been carrying some 500 people, surely many would have been trapped inside and gone with her to the bottom, and so many more skeletons would have been found than has been the case.

3. *The Court of Inquiry*

The fate of *Vasa*, this inexplicable catastrophe, caused a tremendous stir and was a matter of great concern and grief to the people of the capital and, as the news spread, of the whole country. A grave mistake must have been made somewhere, it was felt, otherwise no ship could go down as *Vasa* had. One can imagine that for a while this disaster must have over-shadowed people's lives and been well-nigh the sole topic of conversation in the street and market-place, in inns and even in people's homes. Those of the survivors with a taste for beer and gruesome detail must have found their experiences a ready source of free drinks. In those days news and gossip passed almost exclusively by word of mouth.

Already the day after the disaster, the Council of the Realm began its inquiries. Sitting at the palace, it summoned before it the captain of the ill-fated vessel, who had so narrowly escaped drowning, and *Vasa*'s builder. Captain Söfring Hansson had been arrested, or at least taken to the palace and detained there in custody, almost as soon as he was brought ashore; but after a couple of days he was released against surety.

On 5 September, a proper inquiry began sitting at the palace. A special court was set up to conduct this inquiry and a number of the survivors and others were summoned to appear before it and give evidence. There were seventeen members of the cour , six of them Councillors of the Realm. Admiral Carl Carlsson Gyllenhielm was its president.

Thanks to the researches of the Swedish naval historian, Captain-Commander Georg Hafström, quite a lot is known about the proceedings of this court of inquiry. The official record has not survived, but copies of parts do exist, sufficient to make it possible to judge the causes of the disaster and to reconstruct the proceedings at the inquiry. The techniques of examination and cross-examination do not seem to have been very advanced, and it would appear that the members of the court had no great understanding of the chain of command and responsibility aboard a ship of *Vasa*'s size. Also, it is all too evident that they were out to try to find a scapegoat, and that as quickly as possible. Knowing the severity of the punishments meted out in those days, one cannot but be sorry for the protagonists in this great drama. And one can see that at times the atmosphere in the court must have been ominously charged.

The first person to have anything like a bad time of it was Erik Jönsson, the master of ordnance, whom the king himself had chosen to command the fleet which *Vasa* was to have joined. Where *Vasa*'s handling and manoeuvring were concerned, Jönsson had no real function or responsibility. As an artilleryman, his interest was primarily in the ship's guns and armament. He informed the court that he had in fact inspected *Vasa*'s guns after she had heeled over that first time, that was before sail had been set and she was still lying inshore by the oil sheds, and he had found nothing wrong: all the guns had been properly lashed and secured. When she had heeled over a third time and had begun to capsize, he had run down to the battery-deck again. Water was then already gushing in through the open gun-ports and

21

Jönsson had shouted to the men to pay out the sheets, but that had already been done. The water rose so swiftly inside the ship that the companion-way down to the battery-deck came loose and floated off on its own. The master of ordnance just managed to get up on deck again in the nick of time.

Under examination the king's master of ordnance revealed a considerable lack of confidence in the ship that was to have come under his command. He gave it as his opinion that she would undoubtedly have capsized whether sail had been set or not. Her superstructure was far too bulky and weighty. The ship, he said, 'was heavier over than under'. Here the admiral, president of the court, pointed out that the master of ordnance, being commissioned vice-admiral and aboard a ship which came under his command, ought to have acquainted himself with the state of the ship and whether she was properly ballasted. To this Erik Jönsson replied that he was not a ship's captain or a vice-admiral, and had never pretended to be either. He was a master of ordnance and considered that *Vasa*'s captain and commander should have known more about the ship than he did and been better able to judge whether or not she was correctly ballasted.

In conclusion, the president pointed out that the ship's builder had said that, if he had been informed that the ship was top-heavy, he would have had her loaded down another foot, and asked what the master of ordnance had to say about *that*?

What the master of ordnance had to say was brief, but to the point. How could that have been done, he wanted to know, when the gun-ports were already only three and a half feet above the level of the water?

Then it was the turn of Lieutenant Petter Gierdsson, who had been in charge of rigging *Vasa*. He too had been aboard because he had been ordered to sail with her on her maiden voyage. He was accused straight out of not having informed those concerned that *Vasa* was top-heavy. That, said the lieutenant, was a thing about which he knew nothing. He had had nothing to do with anything but the rigging, and he had not even known what kind of ballast had been put in her. Lieutenant Gierdsson confirmed that all the guns had been well lashed and secured. The gun-ports were about four or four and a half feet above water, he said, and *Vasa*'s draught was fourteen feet for'ard and sixteen feet astern, and fifteen 'shoes' in the bilge. He also informed the court that he would never have thought that any ship could have capsized in so faint a wind. The court then wanted to know whether Gierdsson knew, or had formed any opinion as to the reason why *Vasa* had capsized so easily—was it because she was badly built or had too little ballast? No, Lieutenant Gierdsson had no views on this subject. With modesty that was more than becoming or justifiable, he insisted that he knew nothing about all that, because he had no knowledge or understanding of shipbuilding, nor, he repeated, had he even seen what kind of ballast or how much the ship carried.

The next person on the list was Jöran Matsson, *Vasa*'s master. He must have been a fine fellow and a tough customer. The charge against him was one of real gravity, namely 'that he had failed his calling and his office in that he had not paid due attention to ballast and other things as his calling and office made incumbent upon him, whereby disaster had befallen His Majesty's ship'.

To this *Vasa*'s master replied that he had stowed in as much ballast as there was room for in the bilge. Not only that, but he had personally checked that the men did the work properly by himself going down into the bilge with a light in order to adjust and move and get in as much as was possible. He, Jöran Matsson, certainly considered that he had done his best to carry out his duties and do all that was incumbent upon him.

Then came what was to prove the dramatic moment of the whole inquiry: the master was asked if he had noticed that the ship was top-heavy, prior to the disaster. Matsson's reply was a sensational disclosure. Bluntly he informed the court that, weeks before, Captain Hansson had reported to Admiral Fleming that the new ship was top-heavy. Not only that, the master went on, but when *Vasa* had been lying at the gun-crane with her ballast already aboard, they had made a 'capsizing-test'. With the admiral aboard, they had made thirty men run from one side of the ship to the other. The first time they ran across, *Vasa* had gone over by the breadth of one plank, the second time she had gone over two planks' breadth and the third time, three. The admiral had then ordered them to stop. If they had gone on with the test and made more runs, the admiral had said, 'she would have gone right over'. At that time His Majesty the King had still been at home. And *Vasa* had already taken in the whole of her ballast, except for one small boat-load.

Matsson, however, maintained that even if it were God's will that the ship should be salvaged and she should then be loaded down over the gun-ports, she would still capsize, because she was too narrow-bottomed and had no proper belly. And the dauntless Matsson informed the court that he had told Admiral Fleming as much when they were taking in the ballast, but that the admiral had told him: 'You're carrying too much ballast; the gun-ports are going to be too near the water.' To this Matsson said he had replied: 'God grant that she'll even stay on an even keel.' And the admiral's rejoinder was: 'The builder has built ships before. You don't need to worry like that.'

It is not difficult to imagine the stir this man's evidence must have caused. And how many toes he was treading on!

Matsson then went on to confirm that all the guns had been properly lashed and secured, and he ended with a rhetorical question: if *Vasa* hadn't been able to carry those four small sails in the calm weather that had prevailed at the time of the catastrophe, how could she have carried her topgallants and other sails in a good breeze?

So far, all who had come before the court had been able to clear themselves; but a scapegoat they had to have; so they seized on the bos'n, poor Per Bertilsson. Why, the court wanted to know, had he not seen to the sails and ropes as he ought? Or had he by any chance been drunk? The poor man, with the courage of despair, replied: 'That day I had been at the Lord's Table.' And that was that! The court was still without its scapegoat. So far nobody had been found to have failed in his duty, nobody had been shown to be at fault. Now there was only the ship's builder left and he was the next to appear before the court.

Hein Jacobsson was *Vasa*'s builder, or rather it was he who had completed and delivered her. But he had not laid her keel or begun the work. Thus, when he was asked why he had made *Vasa* narrow, with no belly, and so badly that she had capsized, he had no difficulty in finding an effective reply, one that in fact was almost like a boomerang.

In those days there were, of course, no such things as naval architect's plans or blue-prints. A ship was built according to what was called a 'sert', that is a table giving the most important dimensions of the ship which was being ordered, and this was to some extent also a contract to build. The original builder, Master Henrik, who laid *Vasa*'s keel and started work on the frame, had died in 1627, but the sert had been drawn by this Master Henrik in accordance with the orders of the king himself, and Hein Jacobsson could assert that the ship was built in accordance with this directive. Not only that, but where her 'narrowness' was concerned, she was in fact one foot and five inches broader than had been planned originally. And, he added, 'Everybody says that she was well built.'

Then there was the question of why *Vasa* had been given such a big superstructure, and on this point Arent Hybertsson de Groot, merchant, was questioned; for he was a brother of the original builder, Master Henrik. It must have been a comforting feeling knowing that all criticism could be turned aside by showing that what had been done was in accordance with the orders of His Majesty the King. You could not have a better defence than that. Certainly, de Groot seemed neither overawed nor even much impressed by the solemnity of the court before which he had been summoned. His answer was the same as Hein Jacobsson's: the ship had been built in accordance with the sert agreed by his brother and himself with His Majesty the King. *Vasa* had agreed with the model which he had shown to His Majesty. This was the model of a French ship built in Holland for the Duc de Guise. There had been nothing wrong with *Vasa*, de Groot insisted, and all would have been well, if she had only been ballasted properly.

Ah, but on one occasion, the prosecutor retorted, Hein Jacobsson had said to Captain Hansson that the ship he had built was as tight as St Peter and would be able to sail even without ballast. Jacobsson could not now recollect ever having said such a thing. In fact, he denied it stoutly and again insisted that if *Vasa* had had more ballast, she would never have capsized.

This led to a rather acrimonious series of questions and answers, in the course of which Captain Hansson said very much as the master of ordnance had done earlier, that, if *Vasa* had had more ballast put in her, the scupper-holes would have been under water, and the gun-ports would have been so close to the surface that they would not have been able to use the guns at all. And Captain Hansson went on to say that one could only fear that the same fate would befall *Vasa*'s sister ship which was then being built exactly like *Vasa*. Jacobsson retorted that he could only build what he was ordered to build and according to the measurements given him. At this point, the prosecutor diplomatically intervened and said that he would consult other experts about the matter, to which de Groot retorted that however many ship's builders they invited to look at her, they would all say that she was irreproachably built. This prompted the prosecutor to ask why, if she were 'irreproachably built', had *Vasa* capsized; but that was a question which de Groot and Jacobsson felt they must leave to higher powers to answer. 'They knew not, God must know', was all they could say.

'His Majesty the King was told by me how long and how broad the ship was,' Arent de Groot said, 'and His Majesty was pleased to approve and wished to have it so.'

The prosecutor was not going to accept this, however, and he refused to let the matter rest. He made a number of attempts to trap de Groot and Jacobsson and get through this defence. He devoted a lot of attention to what was a question of the greatest importance and delicacy, namely that, even though His Majesty the King

27

had wished the ship to be built according to the dimensions set out in the sert, should not they, who were entrusted with her construction, have informed the King of what would have been the correct dimensions? Did they, he wanted to know, really consider it compatible with common sense and their consciences to build such a ship as *Vasa*? But neither de Groot nor Jacobsson was to be enticed away from their sure defence of 'the King wished it so'. Again Jacobsson protested that *Vasa* had been as well built as a ship could be. This called forth an immediate and most pertinent retort from the prosecution: 'Of course the ship was well built, but she had not had the correct proportions.'

Again the prosecutor returned to the attack; this time he directed his question to de Groot. 'After His Majesty the King had contracted with you for the building of a ship,' he said, 'ought you not to have consulted with the builder so that the ship should be rightly built, that is to say, built in such a way that His Majesty the King could use her and have profit of her?' But this just elicited the same old answer: de Groot had built the ship to the best of his understanding as he had contracted with the king to do. As far as *Vasa*'s builders were concerned, that was evidently all that there was to it and they were going to admit no further responsibility.

The next, and last, person to be summoned before the court was a man in the king's service, presumably in the admiralty, called Johan Isbrandsson. He must have been, to some extent, in charge of *Vasa*'s construction, because the prosecutor wanted to know why he, one of His Majesty's servants, had not exercised better control of the new ship's construction, so that she had been better built and able to withstand wind and sea? Why had he not spoken out and informed the king in time that the

28

part of the ship above water was heavier than the part below the water-line?

Isbrandsson replied that, as far as his understanding of the art of shipbuilding went, he considered that *Vasa* had been well built and with all sail set ought to have been able to go to sea. He had not been able to discover any fault in her. He also put forward another point, namely that *Vasa* had been as broad in the beam as *Kronan*, another man-of-war. He considered her a good ship, perhaps even stouter than *Kronan*.

That was all very well but, if it had been the case, then why had *Vasa* capsized, the prosecutor wanted to know. Isbrandsson just did not know. It seemed to him quite impossible that such a ship as *Vasa* should have gone over. Finally, Isbrandsson was asked how far above water *Kronan*'s gun-ports were. About four feet, he thought, but to check this a Captain Frans was sent to measure the exact distance.

A reconstruction of how *Vasa* probably looked when ready and fully equipped for her maiden voyage.

1. Mates' quarters
2. Master's quarters
3. Top deck. In the bows and astern of the main-mast, the mouths of cannon look out threateningly from round gun-ports
4. Officers' cabins. The tiller passed through here. As can be seen, this was moved by means of a lever from the cabin-deck, two decks above
5. Upper battery-deck
6. Galley or kitchen
7. Cannon-ball store
8. Lower battery-deck
9. Anchor capstan
10. Pumps
11. Provision store
12. Locker for anchor cables
13. Sail locker
14. After powder-magazine
15. Ballast and water-supply
16. Forward powder-maga-zine
17. Store for ropes and other necessities

4. *No Findings Declared*

The loss of *Vasa* occurred at a critical period in Sweden's history and it was a grievous blow. Financially the blow was considerable, yet the loss to Sweden's defences was even more serious. As early as 1615, the Council of the Realm had found cause to complain that 'the fleet, on which the whole welfare of the realm seemed to depend, had become very neglected and reduced for these times of war', and ever since 1620 fairly intensive efforts had been made to expand the fleet, but losses by enemy action, fire and the hazards of the sea had meant that little more had been achieved than to maintain its numbers at their unsatisfactory strength. It is thus understandable that the government of the day regarded the loss of *Vasa* as a disaster of some gravity.

In mere terms of money, too, the loss must have been a grave one. A man-of-war of *Vasa*'s size, fully equipped, cost about 100,000 *riksdaler*, and to have so much of the wretched taxpayers' hard-earned money literally cast into the sea to no purpose was a tremendous loss, especially at a time when the Treasury as often as not was scraping the bottom of its barrel. The country's finances were then at a very low ebb and wages and salaries could not always be paid on the dot. In fact, there were many occasions when the money to pay those in the king's service was just not there. The fleet, amongst others, was supposed to be paid every month, but due to the chronic lack of money it had become almost a rule that the fleet was paid only a few times a year. It is said that four shipwrights who worked at the naval establishment at Skeppsholmen had been so long without wages that their indignation turned to despair and they ended by refusing to do any more work until they had been paid what they were owed. The result of this desperate challenge was that they were condemned to death for mutiny. This sentence was commuted by the highest instance to one that sounds, and may have been, almost as bad: the four were pardoned and only had to run the gauntlet six times between 260 men! First they were prepared for death and received the last sacrament, so it looks as though the sentence was in actual fact unchanged.

In these circumstances, it is understandable that Captain Söfring Hansson was put under arrest almost as soon as he came ashore; and one can also understand the eagerness of those in high places to set up a court of inquiry and find and punish those who might be responsible. It is thus all the stranger that no findings were ever published and no culprit punished. The reasons are open to conjecture, but one thing at least we know: the members of the court were certainly not fools. We do not know the names of them all, but they included a Privy Councillor, the Chancellor's brother, and other nobles, and also two naval captains, one of whom later became a vice-admiral and the other a lieutenant-admiral, a noted industrialist and the Lord Mayor of Stockholm. The chairman, the stately Lord High Admiral Carl Carlsson Gyllenhielm, half-brother of Gustavus Adolphus II, was no chicken. He had served as a colonel in the Livonian campaign of Charles IX, his father, and had shown courage and considerable military skill. Then he had been taken prisoner and had spent twelve years in Polish prisons, six of them in chains. Though this long period of hardship and captivity had cost him some of his physical and mental powers and flexibility, he was far from being a broken man. In 1619 he was made supreme commander of the navy, a post that he held for nearly ten years, leading the fleet to success on several occasions.

It seems incredible that a court consisting of such men should not have been able to discover the true cause of the disaster. It was true that *Vasa*'s real builder, Master Henrik Hybertsson, had died in 1627 and so could not be made answerable, but in Hein Jacobsson and Master Henrik's brother, they had two men who could be held responsible for the ship's construction.

It is possible that Skipper Matsson's sensational evidence saved those involved from being sentenced and punished, in which case he would have done them a very good turn indeed, for in those days sentences and punishments were anything but mild. If anyone had been considered guilty, he or they would certainly have paid for such dereliction with their lives. According to the naval articles of 1644, for example, a helmsman, who through careless navigation ran his vessel aground, was to be keel-hauled and made to make any damage good. Similarly, a person who by heedless behaviour caused fire to break out aboard ship was to be thrown into the fire he had caused.

But, in the case of *Vasa*, no one was found guilty—or, at least, there is no record anywhere of anyone having been found guilty and sentenced. There is no doubt that Skipper Matsson's evidence put the members of the court in a very awkward and difficult situation, for it all but pinned the responsibility on Admiral Fleming, the Lord High Admiral's right-hand man. The man who built *Vasa* had also succeeded in washing his hands of all responsibility by his insistence that he had only done what the king wanted, no more and no less. If the king in person had arranged and accepted the sert, it made it difficult or impossible for the court to find that the sert had been faulty. Also, as long as *Vasa* lay beneath the waters of Strömmen, no one could prove that there was a fault in her construction.

Had Admiral Fleming kept quiet about what he thought of *Vasa*'s stability out of misguided and misdirected consideration for his master, the king? Or had he not considered that the capsizing-test proved anything? Or had he just hoped that it would all turn out all right in the end?

One will never know why Admiral Fleming, with all his experience, made light of that stability-test, when it showed so clearly that *Vasa* was top-heavy. Was he really in two minds himself? There is a certain amount of contradiction in what he said, at least according to the record of the proceedings of the court of inquiry. According to the master's, Matsson's, evidence, Admiral Fleming ordered Matsson to stop the test 'because', as he said, 'if the men had run across a few more times, she would have gone over', and he had also said that he wished that the king had been at home. But then, a little later, he had told Matsson not to worry about the ship's stability, since those who had built her had built ships before. Evidently the blind faith we have in the authority of the specialist and technician existed even in those days! As far as is known, Fleming never publicly denied, or confirmed Matsson's evidence. Considering how awkward and embarrassing this was, that itself is highly peculiar.

Even though it never published any findings, the *Vasa* inquiry had its repercussions. At that time there were in Sweden a number of foreigners who had contracted to maintain the older vessels of the Swedish Navy, equipping them with what they needed, and to build new ships for the fleet. Among these entrepreneurs were two Scotsmen, brothers, Richard and Hans Clerck, who later entered Swedish service and became admirals. From 1615 to 1628 they had a contract to maintain the rigging in all naval vessels at Stockholm. Among those who built ships for the Swedish Navy were Henrik Hybertsson, whom we know, and in Gothenburg a man called Albrekt von Velden. There were also two men from Holland and one from Brussels, similarly engaged. This system of contracting and sub-contracting had the advantage that it relieved the admiralty of the need to supervise a lot of detail, which was a great advantage, but it had very definite drawbacks too. It was not long after the system was introduced, that it became apparent that several of the contractors were not fulfilling their contracts. Even before the *Vasa* catastrophe, Admiral Fleming had had several occasions to deal with cases of negligence in the equipment of ships. The ships' captains had also complained to the admiral and expressed their dissatisfaction with the system. Even the king had threatened these gentlemen contractors with his displeasure, and in 1628 he lost patience altogether and wrote to Fleming, who was with the fleet lying off Danzig, that he was returning to the capital and was going to see that 'Skeppsholmen and all that went with it was taken properly in hand'. When Admiral Fleming returned, he had a good clear-out among the entrepreneurs, whom he treated with a heavy hand. The whole system of contracting was revised and notice was given that one or two of the biggest contracts—those for maintaining rigging and islands and buildings—were to be terminated at the end of 1628. From 1629 the Crown took over the maintenance of its ships, at least in part, though it still continued to contract with entrepreneurs for the construction of new ones. It is quite possible that *Vasa*'s disastrous maiden voyage helped to hasten this result. It was a bitter lesson of the faults of a bad system, and its repercussions were soon felt. After 1630 they began to build men-of-war broader—but no findings of the court of inquiry have ever been discovered.

5. Salvage Pioneers

Like all tidings of disaster, the news of the catastrophe that had befallen *Vasa* spread swiftly, and it was soon known far beyond the frontiers of Sweden that a new, well-equipped man-of-war had sunk while almost still in the sheltered waters of Stockholm harbour. Responsible men of resource, treasure-seekers, charlatans and adventurers scented easy money. Were there not sixty-four good guns and a well-filled treasure-chest waiting there for those who could get them? For nearly sixty years, to be accurate from 13 August 1628 till August 1683, people fought, quarrelled and strove to get this booty. Contending claimants and those who felt that they had been cheated by partner or associate laid plaint before the Notarius Publicus or sought redress from the courts. Meanwhile, at intervals, more or less fruitless efforts were made to wrest from *Vasa* the precious things still there inside her, only seventeen and a half fathoms, 104 feet, below the surface. One hundred and four feet, that was all. She was as near as that, yet the treasure she carried was inaccessible, remote.

They were a colourful lot, the men who tried their luck and sought to raise *Vasa* or salvage some of her valuables, and they belonged to many nationalities. Before they could try their luck, they had to have the approval of the Privy Council. The list of these applicants starts with an Englishman, then comes a French captain, a Dutch shipwright, a Swede, a man from Lübeck, a Hr. Carl Classon of unknown nationality, a Scots baron, another Scot, a 'mechanicus' from Riga, another Swede, another Englishman, and so it goes on. There were many of them. They intrigued and schemed to get the Council to grant them the privilege of trying to raise sunken ships for the Crown, with *Vasa*, of course, foremost in their minds. The art of diving suddenly became immensely popular, and the privilege-seekers were not afraid of big words when describing their skill and experience in raising even big ships. It is only fair to say that some of them really were competent and had performed wonders. In those days tools and equipment were extremely primitive, technical resources poor; yet they did not shrink from attempting even such an enormous undertaking as raising a ship of several hundred tons. Thanks to the research that has been done, we now know quite a lot about the exciting treasure-seeking that went on in Stockholm harbour during the seventeenth century.

The man who heads the list of treasure-seekers, the Englishman, Ian Bulmer, made an outright attempt to raise *Vasa*. He was quick off the mark, indeed, for he started work three days after the catastrophe. In his pocket he had the first salvage patent ever issued in Sweden. It was not long before he could inform the Council that *Vasa* was lying without list, almost on an even keel. Presumably, her enormous top-hamper had helped to right her as she sank, slowly but inexorably.

One's mind boggles at the idea that these men of 300 years ago seriously tried to raise *Vasa*. They brought boats and big ships above where she was lying and rigged up their 'instruments'. These were grapnels and anchors with which they caught hold of gun-ports and other suitable places; they passed the ropes round windlasses and wound away in the hope of getting the ship up. Sometimes they succeeded, but not with *Vasa*. She was too heavy and all attempts to raise her were doomed to failure.

The king, however, was impatient. He wanted *Vasa* up at once. His impatience infected the Councillors of the Realm, who felt that Bulmer was not working swiftly enough and, as a result, as soon as Willem de Besche reached Stockholm he was entrusted with the difficult task and put in charge of salvage operations. As his assistant he was given *Vasa*'s former captain, Hansson. But *Vasa* defied all their efforts. They couldn't raise her, not even when, that autumn, Admiral Fleming himself took charge of operations. In the end, they came to the conclusion that there was nothing more they could do without divers to help them. That meant, as Fleming pointed out in a letter he wrote to the king in November 1628, sending to Holland for them. However, it was not to Holland that they actually turned, at any rate in the first place. Instead, Henrik Mansson, Governor of Carelia, was ordered to try to find divers who could walk under water. He was empowered to tell them that they were to help try to raise *Vasa* and to promise them good pay.

In July 1629, Admiral Fleming again wrote to the king:

> As far as *Vasa* is concerned, we have been working with all industry, trying to raise her, but until now have accomplished little, the reason for this being partly that the lighters and *Gamla Svärdet* are not themselves powerful enough to bear the weight that is down there, partly that both blocks and chains break just when one is hard at it, and then there is another long wait till everything is repaired and ready again. Now I have had *Nya Svärdet* sent

there to help the others and have had the blocks bound with iron. I have also again fixed seventeen stout hawsers and chains with which this week, if the weather permits, we shall try to see what can be done. There is a heavier weight there than I could ever have supposed.

But not even that helped. They could do nothing, the difficulties were insuperable, and, as far as one can see, the authorities then gave up the idea of making any further attempts on their own.

But there were still many people who were only too eager and willing to try their hand, and a succession of salvage experts came and tried and went again. Each was very jealous of his methods and the Council had to undertake not to disclose any details of them, nor to use them themselves without the consent of their author. For ten years these attempts to raise *Vasa* continued more or less uninterruptedly. Then followed a decade that in this field at least was more or less uneventful. But after 1650, public interest was again focused on *Vasa* when a Scots baron, Colonel Alexander Forbes, who till then had been serving in the Swedish Army, declared himself prepared to try to raise *Vasa* and other sunken ships. Colonel Forbes had just been shipwrecked and lost all his possessions, and that apparently had given birth to a sudden interest in diving and salvage. As he had rendered Sweden good service, he was able to persuade Queen Christina and her advisers to grant him the sole right to carry out salvage work in Swedish waters for a period of twelve years. All such work was to be carried out at his own expense. Not being an expert, Forbes had to get assistants and associates who knew the art. For the first few years he had three associates, one of them being Ian

Bulmer, but here he was unlucky, for all three died before they had had time to carry out a single salvage operation and thus the return for their efforts was meagre in the extreme.

Forbes now tried another way of exploiting his licence and making it pay: he leased the right to raise *Vasa* and *Sophia* to a syndicate. *Sophia* was a Danish flagship which had been sunk in eighteen fathoms off Gothenburg during the Swedish–Danish war of 1643–5. The contract provided for a certain sum to be paid to Forbes in cash within a fortnight of one or either ship being raised. The syndicate also gave a written undertaking to use all industry to get the two ships up and to teach Forbes the methods they used. The syndicate included in its number a Scots diver called Jacob Maule and a Swedish colonel, Hans Albrecht von Treileben.

Things went very slowly, and the only result that could be proved at a subsequent court case was that they had managed to salve a few of *Sophia*'s guns, which Treileben had sold.

Treileben would seem to have been a dangerous fellow to have dealings with, for in quite a short period of time he had outmanœuvred Forbes and jockeyed him out of the picture, even before the period of his patent had expired. Treileben was smart and well aware of the value of good contacts and influential friends and patrons. Of these latter he managed to acquire quite a few and they later supported his application for the privilege to carry out salvage work. He received this sought-after licence in December 1658 (when Forbes's patent really had four years yet to run), this entitling him for the next twenty-one years together with, at the most, twenty assistants to practise salvage. *Vasa*, however, he was not then allowed to touch. She was still Forbes's. But to enable Treileben to buy the necessary material and support himself in the meantime, he was given the right to import and export certain goods free of dues and duty throughout the period of his licence. This must have been a valuable concession. The document granting this privilege assesses its value at 2,400 *riksdaler* a year, but one would hardly be wrong in assuming that in the hands of a smart man, such as Treileben undoubtedly was, such a privilege could be made to yield considerably more.

Treileben now held all the trumps. Not only had he deprived Forbes of the major part of his privileges, but he had also taken his technical expert, for we find that Treileben's group of assistants included Maule, the Scots diving expert. Treileben was evidently a good organizer, energetic and a bit of a slave-driver, for he got down to work almost at once and was soon able to record quite considerable success. The very next year, in the midst of hostilities, he salvaged a number of guns from the Dutch flagship *Brederode*, which had been sunk in Oresund. In the end, however, the enemy forced him to interrupt his work and he had to abandon the Dutch ship for the time being. Then he succeeded in raising a big galliot that had gone down in seven fathoms off Landskrona. He also had people working on the west coast, where in one month they got up fifteen guns out of the Danish flagship *Sophia*, at which Treileben had already had a go, when working for Forbes. Farther down the coast from Gothenburg, at Nidingen, he salvaged a trading vessel of 180 lasts, and in the summer of 1661 his men succeeded in salving quite a number of precious objects out of *Resande Man* (see page 6).

In 1663 a new salvage expert appeared on the scene. This was a man called Andreas Peckell who had learned about diving at Lübeck and seems to have been specially interested in *Vasa*'s valuable guns. Peckell tried to make a working arrangement with Maule—behind Treileben's back, of course. The game of intrigue was in full swing again, as we know from the records of a lawsuit that have been preserved. *Vasa*, however, still remained Forbes's preserve. At first Treileben tried to get Forbes to collaborate with him to exploit the old wreck, but there he failed. Instead, Treileben entered into a no doubt profitable working arrangement with Peckell. Finally, he managed to oust Forbes altogether. Having succeeded in this, he and his associate Peckell were free at last to turn their attention to *Vasa*, which was their preserve at last.

For thirty-five years now, *Vasa* had lain there on the bottom. During that time she had been subjected to pretty rough treatment. Grapnels and anchors had lacerated her sides and superstructure, and all the time, being heavy, she had been sinking deeper and deeper into the slime. Her deck was cluttered with rope and cordage, bits of rigging, old cables, chains and all sorts of things, and thus the first thing Peckell and his men had to do was to clear all this away. They had not yet abandoned the idea of seeing *Vasa* afloat again, but Peckell and Treileben were business men first and foremost and they salvaged in order to make money; thus they wanted a quick return for their efforts. They were out to get up as many things of value as they could in the shortest possible time, and they were even prepared to tear off the main deck and saw through the deck-beams, if that should be necessary.

It was a gigantic undertaking on which these two, Peckell and Treileben, had embarked. But they had drive and initiative, and if anyone could have succeeded, they would have. They and their men seem to have toiled and laboured like beasts. An Italian traveller of those days, Francesco Negri, who happened to reach Stockholm at that time, has given a detailed eye-witness account of their work. This was published in 1700, and as a result we now have a very good idea of their methods and of the tools they used.

It was a lovely autumnal day towards the end of October, with a light breeze blowing, when Negri put out in a small sailing-boat that took him quickly to the place where *Vasa* had capsized and sunk all those years ago. There, for some time, a small barge had been anchored, a clumsy craft, dirty and battered. Round her lay a number of other vessels, big and small. These were the boats the new syndicate of Treileben and Peckell were using in what was to be that century's last attempt but one to salve the *Vasa*. The barge's deck was littered with all sorts of tools and mysterious equipment. There were thick hawsers, blocks and stout lifting-tackle designed to deal with great weights. Their first objective was to try to get up *Vasa*'s valuable bronze guns. These weighed from one to two tons apiece and, it will be understood, stout tackle was required to deal with them. The experienced Andreas Peckell, who was in charge of the work, considered it impossible to raise *Vasa* as she was. First, she had to be freed of her many and heavy guns and then they must try to get some of her ballast out. If they could manage that, the optimistic Peckell said, the rest would be quite simple and they would get the great ship to the surface. To get at the second layer of guns meant tearing off the main deck and cutting away the deck-beams, and this they intended to do using special tools, and in fact did.

The extraordinary and amazing methods being used by the new syndicate had brought numbers of prominent persons to the scene to study what was being done. The two men were using that remarkable invention, the diving-bell, by means of which a man could descend to considerable depths and stay there without risk to himself for half an hour. Treileben had introduced this wonderful invention to Sweden in 1658 and had used it successfully on several ships on the west coast and elsewhere, but this was the first time it had been seen in waters anywhere near the capital. Such an effective tool should have made salvage work on *Vasa* very much easier, but unfortunately the water of Stockholm harbour was not as clear and pure as that off Gothenburg and it was very difficult for the men to see what they were doing. However, it had been felt worth trying the new equipment on *Vasa*. The diving-bell itself had been modified and improved and they had even managed to give the divers effective protection against the cold of the water.

When Negri arrived on the scene, they were just preparing a fresh descent to the wreck. The diver who was to go down was seated on a stool and his fellows were helping him into his heavy equipment. This consisted of, amongst other things, two pairs of leather boots and a stout leather jacket fastened with iron hoops and lashings to make it water-tight. Then, before finally rising laboriously to his feet, the diver put on a cap of ordinary cloth.

The diving-bell, which was standing ready on a small raft moored alongside the barge, was not much to look at. It was made of lead, about four feet high and in shape roughly like a ordinary church bell. It was very heavy and it took two men with block and tackle to manœuvre it. The upper end of the lifting gear was fixed to a couple of stout baulks of timber. It did the job, as the divers of the Swedish Navy demonstrated, using a replica, to the International Congress of Historians that met in Stockholm in 1960.

First, the bell was raised about three feet and the diver

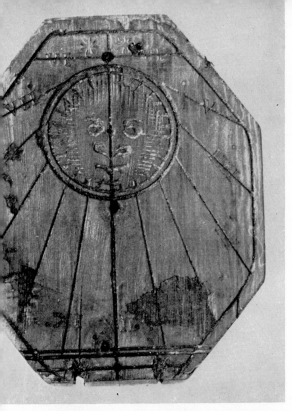

Pocket sun-dial

Small form, about four inches
square, for moulding shot

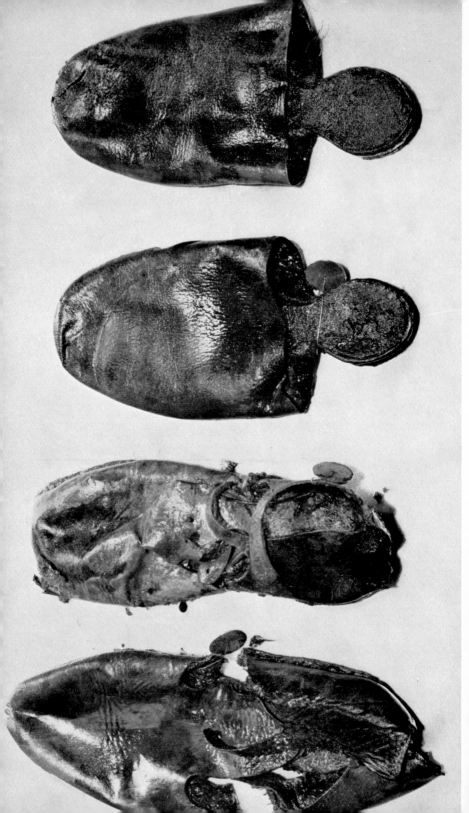

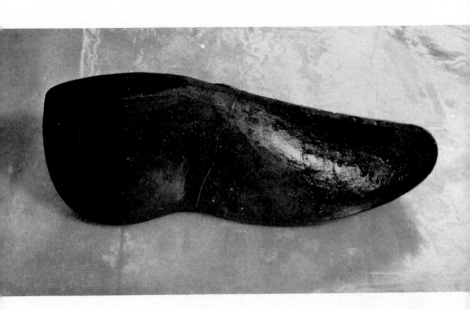

He also had a last . . .

A piece of leather, perhaps for making new shoes . .

A nice pair of gloves . . .

A three-cornered hat,
very well preserved . . .

And a little money

A sewing-box contained, amongst other things, a comb, thimble, thread and some bits of cloth

Beer tankard

Wooden spoon

Brandy keg

Butter keg

Some more household finds: mortar and pestle, tap with the knob shaped like a cock, pottery jar and pewter bottle

bent down and crawled inside, where he stepped up on to a small platform, also made of lead, and suspended by four ropes, twenty inches long, fastened to the inside of the bell. The diver was then handed the tools he was going to need, the most important of these being a six-foot-long, stout wooden pole with a hook at the end, with which the diver could get hold of any object he discovered. There were several different tools for dealing with the heavy guns, great pincers and other things for catching hold and pulling. For anything heavy that had to be lifted up from, or off, the wreck, the diver carried a stout rope in his bell. One end of this was fastened to the raft, the other, free, end could comparatively easily be tied round the object to be lifted.

The guns in the upper and lower battery-decks had to be coaxed out through the gun-ports, but how that could be done the experts were unwilling to reveal. A thin cord for signalling was the diver's only means of communicating with his companions up above.

Once on his little platform inside the bell, the diver gave the signal that he was ready and the bell was pushed out over the water. Then, slowly and carefully, it was lowered into the water.

How could the diver breathe when the water thrust in and filled the bell? That was the ingenious thing about it: the water did not fill the bell. It could not. The air was forced up into the broad upper end of the bell, and being unable to escape, it there formed a cushion of slightly compressed air that prevented the water rising any higher. There the diver stood in the water, his leather clothing protecting his body from the chill, but with his head and neck in the air. By using a special air-store—a barrel fitted with a piece of piping—it had proved possible to extend considerably the time a diver could stay down. The

The seventeenth-century divers did wonderful work with their primitive apparatus. This is a drawing of the diving-bell that Treileben used, showing a diver at work

maximum was said to be half an hour or just over, but the diver Negri saw came up again after about a quarter of an hour. To prove that he really had been down at the wreck he had with him a heavy oaken plank with iron on it. He was shaking with cold, despite his protective clothing and the fact that he was accustomed to the work, so the temperature of the water must have been low indeed.

Naturally, the diving-bell was not without its dangers. It had sometimes happened that the diver slipped off his platform inside the bell and then had considerable difficulty in saving himself. For that reason, they were then experimenting with a sort of saddle on which the diver could sit securely inside the bell, instead of having to stand. Other attempts to improve the equipment had not been so successful. Negri was told of an experiment that had nearly cost one of the divers his life. Peckell had designed a new kind of breathing apparatus, consisting of a long tube or pipe. One of the divers, a man called Anders, was sent down in his protective clothing (but not in the bell) and told to try to breathe through the tube. He had not gone far, however, before he began to suffocate and had to be hauled up to the top again. After that, he took to his bed and stayed there a week, spitting blood and in very poor shape.

Diving in those days was not an enviable occupation. These divers must have been brave men and full of energy, for they did wonders. They managed to get up the majority of *Vasa*'s guns, over fifty of them. (The exact number is not known.) Most of these guns were sold abroad, as we know from the customs records that are still extant. Having been so successful, the syndicate's interest in *Vasa*, which now contained less of value, seems to have cooled and work on her stopped in 1665. Treileben had by then discovered other, and presumably more profitable, fields.

There followed a period of nearly twenty years during which *Vasa* was left in peace, but then another salvage expert appeared on the scene, a man called Liberton, who claimed to have a 'special invention' to offer the king. Liberton asked to be allowed to take over Treileben's licence. His application was granted and in 1683 he began work. He succeeded in getting up one of *Vasa*'s big 24-pounder guns, which, we know, he offered to the government, but the authorities said no thank you, and told him he could sell it to whoever would have it.

That would seem to have been all. No more was heard of *Vasa*, which seems to have been left to sink deeper and deeper into the mire, and in time she became a hump, a mysterious and awkward obstacle in which ships' anchors caught, so that irate captains were forced to cut their cables to get away—losing their anchors.

Fortunately for the historian, these men who tried to raise *Vasa* were as cantankerous as they were colourful. If Forbes and Treileben, Maule and Peckell had not kept quarrelling and taking each other to court, a great deal of this part of *Vasa*'s history would not have been known.

6. *The World-wide Sensation*

Vasa's history is undeniably unique. It comprises little more than two hours' sailing time followed by 330 years lying still and silent at the bottom of the sea: no honourable encounters, no battling with storms, no feats of seamanship, nothing. She never helped to defend Sweden, as she was built to do. All she did was to go down—and come up again. It is a strange fate for a man-of-war to be a cause of dismay and disappointment in her own day, yet to be greeted with enthusiasm and fervour three centuries later; to sink without a shot being fired at her in the day of her country's need and come to life again in the age of space travel. She has sailed through the centuries, bringing with her tidings of many things concerning our forefathers that are of the utmost interest to us today. A strange time-machine indeed.

Vasa is the oldest ship, so far discovered and able to be definitely identified, to be in such good shape. After being raised, she was even able to float on her own keel, even though it was only for a comparatively short time. Also, she belongs to a period of shipbuilding about which we know very little.

The nearest approach to *Vasa* is Nelson's famous flagship at the battle of Trafalgar; but *Victory*'s keel was laid a good 130 years later than *Vasa*'s. There are, of course, very much older ships that have been found or discovered, but these have been either ceremonial or funeral ships, thus not intended for ordinary use. Nor has it been possible to name and date them, as is the case with *Vasa*. Take, for example, the so-called Caligula's galleys: these floating palaces were 220 feet long and 65 feet wide, and were probably built by Caligula (A.D. 12–41) and used for the entertainment of the emperor and his friends on Lake Nemi, a crater lake in the Albano hills just outside Rome. For hundreds of years these galleys tempted treasure-seekers and fired the imagination of the archæologists and historians of Rome. Then, Mussolini had the two vessels salvaged, by the simple and radical expedient of draining the entire lake, which was 112 feet deep and covered an area of $64\frac{1}{2}$ square miles. The ships were laid bare and removed, together with other finds, to a museum specially built for them near the lake. There the Germans burned them in the spring of 1944.

One of the museums at Bygdöy outside Oslo houses two reconstructed ships from the days of the Vikings, the Gokstad and the Oseberg ships. Both these were discovered ashore in great tumuli. They are considered to have been built about the ninth or tenth century.

But of ships built to sail and serve as other ships do, there is only *Vasa*.

The first sign of life that *Vasa* gave in this century was a small piece of black oak—the reward that crowned a lengthy and laborious search. This little piece of oak was like a clarion call and it made those in authority realize that in all probability the lost ship had been found. Naval divers went down and were soon able to provide proof that this assumption was correct: *Vasa* had been found. That was in 1957.

At that time, the picture was this: it was known that

    1. *Vasa* was built of oak and that in all probability

the more important parts of her hull were intact.

2. She had been armed with forty-eight bronze 24-pounder guns which would not corrode.
3. She was a royal ship and had sunk on her maiden voyage in 1628 with all her equipment.
4. She had gone down quickly, quite undamaged and with everything still aboard.
5. She was lying on an even keel on firm clay.
6. She had been well preserved by layers of mud and ooze.
7. She had never been exposed to the harmful effects of ice-pressure, swell, vegetable or animal life, short-wave light-rays or free oxygen.
8. She lay close to the naval dockyard, whose considerable resources could be used on her independently of wind and weather.
9. She could be identified with absolute certainty.
10. In all probability she was the oldest ship so far found in such good condition that could be dated and named.

Thus, in many ways, conditions have favoured *Vasa*. Her discovery was a world sensation and gave rise to great anxiety in many spheres; but the step from discovery to raising was long and fraught with many difficulties.

A variety of questions had to be answered before it was possible even to consider raising the sunken ship. What was her shape? How was she lying? Would her hull stand being lifted? What would they do with her, if they did manage to raise her? How could she be protected and saved from being ruined by sun and wind, once she was up? Where was the money for this costly operation to come from? Who would pay for a museum for her? And so on.

To answer these questions and take charge of the whole

project a special *Vasa* Committee was appointed in February 1957 under the chairmanship of Commodore Edward Clason. The committee's first task was to investigate the technical and financial aspects of the undertaking. As well as being a big undertaking, it was also a highly complicated one that called for scientific knowledge and organizing skill of high quality, to say nothing of practical seamanship. The naval authorities were admirably prompt in providing assistance. Amongst other things, much of the training of naval divers was reorganized so that it could be carried out on *Vasa*, with the result that most divers in the Swedish Navy are now very familiar with their service's oldest ship. They and their training were in charge of P. E. Fälting, who altogether has spent one and half years, of the fifty he has so far lived, under water.

The one question that overshadowed all others, of course, was: could she be got up? Before this could be answered, she had to be inspected and measured as accurately as possible. This proved an exceedingly difficult task and one that took a great deal of time; but little by little the requisite information was obtained. It was then known that the depth down to *Vasa*'s keel was just over 118 feet; while there were ninety-four to ninety-eight feet of water on her port side and 100 to 104 feet on her starboard side. The more or less firm clay bottom was covered with a layer of mud and slime six to ten feet deep. The relatively deep water in which *Vasa* was lying helped to make the work more difficult. The time it takes to bring a diver up to the surface—a gradual process—is directly related to the depth in which he has been working. For example, a diver who has been down at 100 to 110 feet for from thirty-five to fifty-five minutes, must take about forty-eight minutes over his ascent to the surface, while if he has spent only twenty to thirty-five minutes at this depth, he will require no more than seventeen minutes. It was because of this that, in order to save working time by keeping the time of ascent as low as practicable, it was decided, as a rule, to restrict each diver's working time on the wreck to about half an hour.

Visibility down at the wreck was very bad. The water in that part of Stockholm harbour is so muddy that to all intents and purposes no light penetrates below sixteen to twenty-two feet. How bad this is will be recognized, when it is realized that in the clear waters of a mountain lake as much as thirty per cent of the daylight can be left even at 100 feet. On certain days, by using 1,000-watt diver's lamps, the divers working on *Vasa* were able to see up to five feet in front of them, when 100 feet down; yet the moment they began to work, they stirred up the slime and mud, which swirled up round them in clouds making it impossible to see anything. The particles of mud and impurities in the water reflect and disperse light, thus making even the 1,000-watt lamps useless. All the divers saw was a greyish white wall in front of them. It was the same thing as happens when you switch on the headlights of a car in fog or when snow is falling thickly. Because of this bad visibility no one actually saw *Vasa* as a whole until she was put into dry dock in 1961. The divers had to grope their way about the torn and riven deck and feel where the gun-ports were, half choked with mud. They glimpsed stumps of masts, caught glimpses of the ship's fantastic ornamentation, stumbled over loose objects lying beside the hull—but they saw very little. What they did see was at once reported back by telephone, and the news broadcast by loudspeaker, so that all in the divers' boat could follow what was going on. Every little

E

fact was noted on sketches and plans. In time, the divers became familiar with the wreck despite these difficulties, and after a while their telephoned reports were in the style of the following:

'I am at point 4 and making towards the stern. Here is the fallen-in cross bulkhead. This is where the forecastle ends. Here is point 8.'

Even so, it was extremely difficult to obtain a true picture of the old ship. It was like a jigsaw puzzle and in order to get the pieces to fit and avoid gaps, the divers' work had to be co-ordinated and methodical.

It soon became obvious that there must be some base, a point of departure for measurements and observations. This was obtained by fixing plastic cords, marked off in metres, from the bow along both rails. This could not provide really accurate measurements, but it was a good idea and served its purpose. This business of measuring the wreck took a whole month of patient work.

The next step was to check the deck-beams, which involved examining every one of them. This was important because on their strength and solidity largely depended whether or not it would be possible to raise the ship in one piece. In the bad visibility down there it was only too easy to lose one's sense of direction and so each beam, starting in the bows, was numbered with big figures at its either end, so that the divers could be sure that they really had followed the same beam right across the ship. This simple sounding job took a further month to complete. These measurements showed that *Vasa* had no list worth speaking of.

Next, the gun-ports were counted. Not even that was easy.

In one of the committee's early reports there is the following:

The number of gun-ports on the starboard side
was first made to be eleven in the upper battery
and thirteen in the lower. Later, a twelfth gun-port
was found in the upper battery on the port side,
while the thirteenth in the lower battery could not
be found. This may be because the divers, when
counting the starboard gun-ports, confused upper
and lower battery when right at the stern. But it is
by no means out of the question that there may be
closed gun-ports which have so far escaped discovery. In the meantime, however, one must
assume that there are twelve gun-ports in either
battery. In addition there are two ports in the lower
battery in the stern, one on either side of the stern-
post.

Time was marching on, and it was already near the
end of July. It was felt that it was now high time to
investigate the wreck's mud-covered interior as far as the
upper battery-deck. For this an area just forward of the
mainmast was chosen, and this was cleared of mud with
the help of an enormous pump. This stage again required
almost a month to complete, for it was the end of
August before they stopped using the pump.

These months of work had brought the committee a
good step towards the elusive goal of salving the entire
ship. They now had quite a good idea of how the ship
looked, which was essential for any salvage work, and
the committee was able to send out a sketch of her with
its first report. This was probably the first sketch ever
made of her, because in the days when she was built
they used neither sketches nor plans to work on. The
'sert' mentioned earlier was merely a set of measurements
in tabulated form. That was all they had.

The measurements the divers had taken showed *Vasa*'s length to be 162 feet. The longest deck-beams measured twenty-six feet between the rail-posts. The curve of her sides gave a bulge of six feet on either side. When one added the thickness of the two rails, it made the ship over thirty-nine feet broad at her widest point. On the basis of these new measurements and what old information they had, the experts of the Maritime Museum were able to calculate *Vasa*'s approximate weight. They came to the conclusion that she must have a displacement of some 1,300 tons and weigh about 750 tons where she lay.

It was now known that *Vasa*'s hull was in pretty good shape, though the years had left it with some weak spots, and also a satisfactory answer had been obtained to that most important question of the old ship's robustness and the state of her timbers. The divers' examination had showed that she was very stoutly built. All parts on which any strain would be likely to be put, if she were to be raised, were made of oak, and the timbers were in amazingly good condition. There was only a slight superficial softening. A chain, however, is only as strong as its weakest link, so that though the material of which the hull was built might be stout enough, a lot would also depend on how the different parts were joined together. The shipwrights of the seventeenth century proved to have used both wood and iron to put the hull together. A large number of wooden nails (oak and juniper) had been used, but at various points there were also iron bindings, hinges and pins. As far as could be seen, the iron had not come so well out of it as had the wood and was an uncertain factor, doubly uncertain because it was not known how many of these iron ties had been used in the hull.

7. *If and How?*

Was it going to be worth trying? That was what everyone wanted to know. Would it be worth the tremendous effort of organizing such a great salvage operation as would be necessary in order to raise *Vasa*? Would she stand up to the stresses and strains of being lifted? Or would the wires cut her to pieces or perhaps squeeze her sides in? Would the clay even let go of its prey? Or would it not be better and safer, carefully and slowly to take her to pieces there on the bottom, and then put her together again? That would avoid all risk, but *Vasa* rebuilt would not be the same as *Vasa* as she went down. All these questions had to be decided now—before the next step was taken.

As far as could be ascertained there was nothing much wrong with the ship's timbers, despite the fact that she had lain at the bottom of the sea for over 300 years. It was known, too, that the wood that had been embedded in clay had suffered least and that the wooden nails used still had considerable toughness. Then the Institute for Timber Research provided expert evidence which helped to confirm the view that *Vasa* could be raised. According to this expert opinion the ability of her oak to withstand bending, pulling and sideways pressure had been reduced by only some forty per cent. Its ability to stand up to vertical blows, however, was roughly a quarter that of fresh oak.

All these data and opinions had to be weighed, tested

and discussed, but finally the committee came to the conclusion that it could recommend trying to raise *Vasa* as she was. The next thing to be discussed and decided was the method to be used. Among those suggested was that of putting a suitable number of large balloons made of nylon or synthetic rubber inside the hull. These balloons could then be inflated from a pumping-station on the surface. This was a method that the American Navy had used when raising craft sunk in connexion with the Bikini experiments. The method had proved successful and balloons were available with lifting-powers of fifteen, twenty-five and forty tons. The seeming simplicity of the method was deceptive, but those who suggested it had not properly grasped the committee's problem. The balloon method involved the very thing that it was most wanted to avoid, namely considerable force being exerted outwards from within. Ships are built in the first place to withstand considerable force and pressure exerted inward from outside, not the other way round. In fact everything seemed to point to more conventional salvage methods being employed.

This meant using either a sunken pontoon and strong wires or caissons.

There are three principal ways of raising a sunken ship by this conventional method. It can be raised by big air-cylinders which are filled with water and sunk alongside the wreck, to whose sides they are then fastened with chains and wires, after which compressed air is used to expel the water from the cylinders, which then float up to the surface taking the sunken ship with them. Here the lift is made in one stage and there is very little possibility of seeing or controlling what happens down on the bottom.

Where *Vasa* was concerned, it was of the utmost im-

Vasa was a big ship, as can be seen by this scale-drawing of her and of the biggest ship the Swedish Navy has ever had, the cruiser *Göta Lejon*, which is 568 feet long

portance that those working on her should never lose control of what happened under water, and there was considerably more chance of being able to do this, if one or other of the alternative methods was employed. These make use of big pontoons with considerable lifting-power. These pontoons are filled with water until the decks are almost level with the surface, then the big lifting-wires, which have already been passed under the wreck, are fastened round the pontoons in such a way that the pull is distributed and not concentrated on one spot. That done, you start pumping the water out of the pontoons, which rise and take the sunken ship with them. The whole lot— pontoons and wreck—is then towed into shallower water. When the ship hanging in the wires grounds, the process is repeated: the pontoons are submerged, the wires pulled taut and the water pumped out of the pontoons. This process has to be repeated as often as is necessary to get the ship to where it is wanted to have her.

61

With the third variant of this method, it is hydraulic hoisting-gear or screw-jacks that do the actual lifting. The pontoons are fitted with stands for these screw-jacks and have wells down the centre through which the chains run. The chains are shackled to attachments on the wires and made taut with powerful screw-blocks, after which the ship is 'pumped' up in one stage. Whichever of these methods is used, the ship has to be put on the bottom, when nearing the surface, so that the pontoons can be removed.

Where *Vasa* was concerned, there were certain disadvantages about the successive method with its lift and lift again. In the first place, it would not be easy to find expanses of bottom on which *Vasa* could be rested without risk. Big stones, wrecks or other large objects could all too easily harm her precious hull, and the course of her road to safety would have to be most carefully reconnoitred. Another requirement was that the pontoons, whose lift was limited, should in the first place be able to raise *Vasa* out of the deep hole in which she had lain all those years. One of the disadvantages of the screw-jack method was that it called for especially stout lifting-wires with rather clumsy couplings and it might prove difficult to get these under the ship. The distance between the sternmost and foremost jacks would be only seventy-eight feet and that was a considerable drawback. *Vasa* was close on 160 feet in length and thus two large sections of the hull would project beyond the wires and have no support. In such an event, there was a considerable risk that these 'overhangs' might break off. Another, lesser, disadvantage of the hydraulic jack was that a considerable number of hands was needed to work them, for they have to be pumped up by hand. In the end, the committee decided to use the step-by-step method. If this ran into difficulties, it would still be much easier to get the heavy hawsers used with the jacks under *Vasa*, if she had been raised a bit already and was hanging free in the lifting-wires.

While the choice of method and the various technical problems were being discussed, work on the wreck continued without interruption. At the end of August 1959, they began digging the first experimental tunnel under the ship. This was by no means an easy task. In the first place, the old ship could not have sunk in a worse place, for she lay just out from the gates of Stockholm's largest dry dock, and at the end of summer the traffic in and out of the dock was considerable. Ships kept going in for brief periods—and coming out again. Every time a ship went in—or came out—work on *Vasa* had to be interrupted and the divers' rafts towed out of the way. The tunnelling necessitated pumping the mud away in order to get down to the firm clay, and while this was being done, a number of loose objects was found, which had to be freed and dealt with, all of which delayed the actual business of tunnelling. These were not the first objects to be found. A number of things of interest had already been discovered and brought up, among them *Vasa*'s broken foremast, which was recovered in November 1956.

The divers continued tunnelling well into December. It was a laborious business and at this date they had only got as far as the keel, but that was enough, for what they saw made it seem definite that it was going to be technically possible to salvage *Vasa*.

The enthusiasts were convinced that *Vasa* was coming up. She just had to. And to help make this possible, assistance was promised—and given—from all over the country and many places outside Sweden. The big Neptune Company offered to give free use of its two big pontoons, *Oden* and *Frigg*, as well as of a steam-driven salvage vessel. All they asked for was that what they had to pay the divers, and any overtime for the crews, should be refunded. It was a generous offer to which only two small conditions were attached: that *Vasa* should be raised whole and preserved, and that the raising should be carried out by the firm, whose Captain Hedberg should be in charge of operations. Another magnificent offer came from Fagersta Bruk which promised to provide free the twelve six-inch wires, each 390 feet long, which would be needed to raise *Vasa*.

Winter stopped all further work on *Vasa*, but by as early as the middle of April it had been resumed. The task facing the divers was that of boring tunnel after tunnel under *Vasa*'s keel. Here they had to work in what was as good as complete darkness. One man worked from either side and very careful measurements had to be made to ensure that the two tunnels met. The divers could use neither shovels nor spades. Air and water were their tools, a Zetterström nozzle and a big evacuating-pump, whose huge suction-pipe performed very much the functions of a submarine vacuum-cleaner. The nozzle could be adjusted so that the action of the jet was either forward, when it drilled out the mud and clay, or backward, when it cleared the mud away. The diver could adjust it as he liked. The pressure of the jet was constant at about eight to nine pounds. When the jet was directed backwards, it could not be too strong, else the mud and clay would be swept past the mouth of the suction-pipe, whose job it was to remove it. When the first experimental tests were made with this equipment, they used rigid steel tubes which were found to be difficult and awkward to handle. When these were replaced with rubber tubes, the work progressed much more quickly.

One of the hardest jobs was that of making the tunnels underneath *Vasa*'s keel. Here is one of the divers at work, 120 feet down, using his Zetterström nozzle to wash the mud away. The loose mud is quickly removed by the huge suction-tube

Not only that, but the rubber tubes were much easier to take up and put down again, as had to be done each time work was interrupted and the rafts towed away, because a ship was wanting to go in or out of the dry dock.

The divers were naval men. Their suits weighed about 220 pounds, for stout materials and warm woollen clothes were needed when working at a depth of 130 feet or so, where the temperature was only 4°C. The clothes had to be thick also, in order to protect the wearer from chafing, as well as the cold. The actual diver's suit is of strong calico interlined with rubber and made in one piece, so that the wearer has to ease himself into it from above.

65

Rubber cuffs make it water-tight at the wrists. At the neck are two collars, the outer of which is made of stout rubber which is fastened to the so-called breastplate. In the helmet are a connexion for the air-pipe, a regulating valve and a socket for the telephone cable. The valve allows the diver to regulate the amount of air in his helmet. When expertly used, a diver can keep himself floating free in the water just by regulating the amount of air in his helmet.

One of the men had just been dressed and was standing ready. Ungainly, he waddled in his heavy boots across the deck to the ladder. The signal-line with its built-in telephone cable was fastened round his waist and the air-tube was as it should be. The front window of the helmet was closed and screwed up. Air-supply and telephone were given one last test. A tap on the helmet told the man that all was in order. He plumped into the water and began his descent, moving down along the ground-line which led him straight to his place of work 130 feet below. He had the Zetterström nozzle on its tube with him.

It grew dark swiftly as he descended. First, all was green, then grey-green, then dirty brown. Darker and darker it became, until the diver was as good as blind. There was the shaft they had dug, some sixteen feet into the mud and ooze, then the bend in the shaft where it went into the horizontal plane. Slowly and carefully the diver made his way in. This was the tunnel. He groped his way forward to where the last man had stopped work.

Up on the divers' raft, Fälting, the foreman, was following all that went on. The battery meter showed a depth of 120 feet. The diver's voice and breathing were audible through the telephone the whole time. You

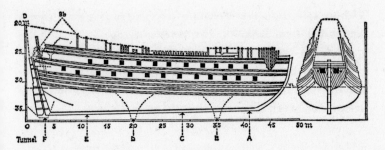

Drawing of *Vasa* made by Commander Edward Clason from the examination and measurements taken by the divers during 1958. The letters A to F show the position of the different tunnels under her keel

could almost tell by his voice that it was uncomfortable down there—and lonely. Nor, of course, was it altogether free of risk. But he and his companions were making progress. The Zetterström nozzle did the job. The clay was loosened and sucked into the wide mouth of the suction-pipe, the other end of which was up on the deck of one of the attendant lighters. There the water gushing from the pipe was carefully scrutinized: smaller loose objects might be brought up along with the mud and clay.

So, little by little, the divers worked their way forward. They had to lie on their stomachs to work and every now and again their helmets brushed against something hard: the bottom of *Vasa*. The old ship, 700 tons of her, was there just above their heads. It was a nasty job, a strain on both nerves and body. But if *Vasa* was to come up, the tunnels had to be made, six narrow tunnels right under her from one side to the other, each nearly eighty feet long. That made nearly 500 feet of tunnel they had to make, working at a depth that varied between

67

114 to 130 feet, before the lifting-wires could be passed under the keel between the pontoons.

In 1958 work on *Vasa* continued almost until Christmas, for it did not stop until 16 December. By that time the divers had together made almost 1,000 descents since systematic work began in the spring of 1957.

8. *The Salvage Fleet Arrives*

Again it was spring, the third spring of salvage operations, and the decisive one. Those in charge were optimistic with an undertone of anxiety. First, the tunnelling
was to be continued and the naval divers who were going
to complete the process were already available for what
was one of the trickiest tasks in the history of salvage.

It is difficult for the ordinary person, the layman, to
understand what a real feat the raising of *Vasa* was. Of
course, many seemingly hopeless ships have been raised;
divers and salvage crews have struggled in the worst
possible conditions to save ships and trapped crews—and
succeeded. Divers have gone down to great depths and
rescued many things of value. Ships have been raised on
open coasts, and harbours cleared of ships sunk in raids
during the war. Human lives and large sums of money
have been staked on salvage attempts. It is the salvage
man's lot to work in silent waters, hard laborious work
that can reward him handsomely, but does not always do
so. Yet the raising of the *Vasa* was unique.

What made it unique was this: normally the salvage
man works on ships about which he knows everything,
at least all that he needs to know. He has blue-prints of
the hull and interior, he knows the dimensions of ribs
and plates, keel and floor-timbers; all the technical details
are known. He knows what the material is capable of
standing, what stresses and strains it will endure without

breaking. Should some of these facts not be available, they can be calculated with reasonable certainty. The diver will even have a plan showing how the cargo was stowed.

But with *Vasa* it was all quite different. There were no plans of her. None had ever been made. That was not done till the end of the eighteenth century. At first nothing was known about the materials used in building her. It was possible to examine parts of the hull, but not others. The heavy stone ballast she carried could not be unloaded because it was impossible to get inside the old ship. No one knew where her centre of gravity lay. They did not even know her exact weight under water. Slime, clay, wretched visibility and constant interruption because of the traffic in and out of the nearby dock were all added, though perhaps minor, difficulties. Not knowing what *Vasa* would stand up to, they were compelled to be most cautious and choose the safest method of raising her. If they had known at the start that the old ship was so resilient and able to stand up to so much more than they had supposed, they could have used quicker ways of getting her up. As it was, they had to anticipate the worst and act with the utmost caution.

The divers were full of enthusiasm and worked hard, almost to the limits of physical endurance. Then the day came, when the lifting-wires lay in place under the old ship's keel, ready to be fixed to the big lifting-pontoons. The day was at hand—after three years' intense work. On 13 August 1959, the units of the salvage fleet began to arrive: *Oden* and *Frigg*, the Neptune Company's two big pontoons with a joint lifting-capacity of 2,400 tons. They were not much to look at, but that was not their function. Their function was just to be filled with water and have it pumped out again once the stout lifting-cables had been fastened in place, thus bringing the sunken ship with them as they rose; that is to say, provided it did not prove too heavy or was caught in the mud and stuck fast. The pontoons had no boiler of their own. The steam that drove their powerful pumps was provided by a vessel lying alongside.

As well as the two pontoons, there was the Neptune Company's salvage vessels *Sleipner* and *Atlas* and the naval tender *Sprängaren*. Above *Vasa* were four stout pontoons and the naval dockyard's divers' boat.

There were now sixty men in the salvage team, headed by Captain Hedberg. One by one the lifting-cables were taken up and fixed to the pontoons in such a way that the pull was evenly distributed. Each cable had to be hauled exactly as taut as the others, otherwise the whole undertaking would be jeopardized. The experts had calculated *Vasa*'s weight under water and worked out where her centre of gravity probably lay. Later, these calculations proved amazingly accurate.

The lifting-wires were 390 feet long and capable of standing a strain of as many tons. Their diameter was two inches and each weighed 125·66 pounds, not easy things to handle and pull taut.

The little salvage fleet was anchored in exactly calculated positions and light buoys put out round it to keep ships and boats from coming too near. Orders were issued restricting boat-traffic in the vicinity of the scene of operations. Private owners of motor- and speed-boats were also told to be very careful, if passing anywhere near, since anything of a wash would jeopardize the work.

These last preparations took a week. Excitement was now intense. In Stockholm people spoke of little but *Vasa*. As a topic of conversation the old ship overshadowed political crises and world events. *Vasa* was herself a world event. Was she, built in the seventeenth century, going

F

to defy the efforts and resources of the twentieth century, or would she behave nicely and let herself be raised? Or would she fall to pieces in the wires? That could happen, and the great question was: what would 'the old 'un', as the divers had long since come to call her, do?

Then 20 August 1959 came—the Day. The men of the salvage fleet were early astir. The wires were checked a final time and divers went down to make sure that all was well with *Vasa* there below. Police boats patrolled the area, stopping craft that were coming too fast and keeping the inquisitive at a distance. At half past eleven all was ready: there were twelve steel wires looped round *Vasa* and hauled taut. The sun blazed down on the assembled salvage men, journalists and prominent personalities come to watch.

Then there was a pause for lunch. Immediately afterwards, the pontoons' pumps began to work. The excitement rose and involuntarily people spoke in hushed voices. Silence reigned as the pumps worked away. A slight quiver in the pontoons' hulls and hissing jets of steam from the pumps were the only signs that anything was happening. Slowly and carefully the two pontoons were emptied, and progressively their lifting-power increased. After about twenty minutes their lifting-power was 100 tons (*Vasa* was thought to weigh about 700 tons). The wires were very taut. It was time to tighten the nuts on the clamps holding them, since the great strain on the wires reduced their size somewhat.

Pumping continued. Crowds had collected at every point on shore from which the operations could be watched. There must have been many more than saw her go down to watch her being brought up off the bottom, the population of Stockholm having increased roughly a hundredfold in the meantime.

At first, there was nothing to be felt or observed on the pontoons. It was in the depths down below them that the dramatic tug-of-war was taking place, though probably there was little to be seen even there. One of the journalists, a woman, expressed a wish that she could have been down there to see and was told by one of the divers: 'You might just as well go into a dark cupboard and feel a bit of wet wood.'

Every now and again the wires' fastenings were checked and the rise of water in the pontoons measured. The divers, idle now, sat on their raft staring intently at the floats of the ground-lines which had been fastened to *Vasa*'s stem and stern in order to show if she moved. After an hour or so the pontoon on *Vasa*'s starboard side began to rise slightly, becoming higher than the port pontoon. Some while later, the port pontoon had a slight list in towards the wreck. And the two pontons had now moved closer together.

That the port pontoon should be inclined inwards was perfectly natural. When *Vasa* sank, she had the wind on her starboard side, and so had heeled over to port. In all probability her ballast had shifted as she capsized and much of it must have rolled over to the port side. There, presumably, it still was and that would make the ship heavier on the port side than on the starboard side, even though she was more or less on an even keel.

The pumps went on working. By a quarter to three, the pontoons' lifting-power had increased to 400 tons. At half past three it was 600 tons and at ten minutes past four it had reached 700 tons, roughly *Vasa*'s presumed weight. Half an hour later they stopped pumping. This was it!

If the calculations were roughly correct and *Vasa*'s weight under water was about 700 tons, the pontoons would now be able to raise her. All was quiet and still. Nothing unforeseen had happened. The wires were still taut like bow-strings, which showed that the *Vasa*'s hull was standing up to the strain. Some bubbles reaching the surface were the only evidence of the silent struggle going on 130 feet below. The clay was unwilling to release its grip. But the lifting-power of the two pontoons could be increased considerably yet. The bubbles showed that the water had begun to seep in between the wreck and her clay-bed so that the suction was slowly but surely becoming less and less. All at once the ground-lines slackened slightly and the floats gave a little bob.

That movement showed that at last it was time to send a diver down to see what had happened there below. One man was sitting on the divers' raft ready but for his helmet. This was now put on and screwed tight. The telephone cable was connected, the air-tube tested, and slowly the diver descended. A short while later the man's voice was heard over the loudspeaker:

'I'm down at the bottom now and can feel the stern-post. According to my measurement *Vasa* has lifted about eighteen or twenty inches. She seems to have taken a bit of a knock at the stern. She lost a splinter or two. The wires have cut a few planks, but otherwise she seems fine.'

By eight o'clock that evening the two pontoons were empty. All the water had been pumped out. The old ship was up, up out of the hole where she had lain for 331 years to the day. Her voyage to her next resting-place could begin.

First, the whole fleet of salvage craft was given a half turn, so that the precious burden cradled in the wires lay athwart the hole out of which she had been raised. This done, they began to tow her away. After about 100 yards

Vasa touched bottom and with the utmost caution was let down on to it. Having got so far, it was decided to call it a day. And what a day it had been!

Vasa's new voyage lasted twenty-eight days and took her 600 yards. The distance she could be taken each day was very short, but each day saw progress made. Each day she was towed a little farther into shallower water; when she touched bottom, *Oden* and *Frigg* were slowly flooded till *Vasa* was resting properly on the bottom, then the cables were hauled tight and fixed in their new position. That done, the water was once more pumped out of the pontoons, raising *Vasa* some thirteen feet. Then on she was towed, till she touched ground once more, when the process began all over again. Once or twice when *Vasa* was let down, she sank more than thirteen feet into soft mud on the bottom so that the next lift got them little or no farther on.

To begin with they towed *Vasa* with her forepart pointing in the direction in which they were going, but after a couple of days, it was realized that this was wrong. *Vasa* was broad and heavy in front, and every time she touched bottom, she scuffled up great piles of mud in front of her and dug herself in deeper than was necessary. So, when she was raised the third time, they decided to turn her right round and tow her stern first. When *Vasa* was first raised, she had a list of ten or twelve degrees and was slightly down in the head, but those two details were quickly corrected.

Though there were difficulties, nothing seriously untoward or dramatic happened whilst the old ship was being towed. The only things that happened were that when she was being towed the cables tended to shift and the divers had a difficult job putting them back in place. One day bad weather made it impossible to move her at all, so the opportunity was taken to send divers down to go over the wires once again and they also put a further wire in place round her.

The ground *Vasa* rested on at each stage sloped. Hers was an uphill journey, so to speak, because she was being taken into shallow water. Because of this, and the fact that her bottom was slippery, she had a tendency to slip in her wires, as though trying to escape. And then, towards the end of her journey, the lift had to be made most carefully in order to prevent her knocking against the pontoons. A further difficulty was that at one point they had to negotiate *Vasa* through a confusion of anchor-chains and mooring-cables, a nerve-racking business for those in charge. But all went well and on the afternoon of Wednesday, 16 September, they could report that the first stage of her salvage had been accomplished successfully.

By this time the navy's divers had made 1,300 descents without incident or accident, which says a lot for their skill and the knowledge of those who trained them.

9. *The Early Finds*

Numbers of finds were made during the three years of preparing for the final lift, and by the autumn of 1959 they numbered some 800.* Of these, forty-six were found when making tunnel A, forty-five at tunnel B, tunnel C produced nineteen, tunnel D 139 and E fifty-four. F, the shaft made under the stern, yielded no less than 388. The earliest finds tended to stimulate rather than satisfy curiosity. The list is headed by a very ordinary 'Deal plank, rounded on one side, flat on the other. Length 9·80 m. Breadth 55 cm., tapering'; but the first object to be salvaged from *Vasa* in modern times was brought up in November 1956; this was the ship's foremast, a slimy stout pole nearly sixty-five feet long. Later, the upper part of the lower section of the mast was also found, and this enabled the experts to state that the whole mast had been eighty feet. At deck-level its diameter was nearly thirty inches.

But it was not long before some real titbits were being pulled up out of the mud beside the old ship. A series of really beautiful wood-carvings showed that *Vasa* actually had been a kingly ship. We still know very little about this art-form in the seventeenth century, how extensively it was practised and to what uses it was put, but we do

* This, of course, was before the archæologists had properly started work. Their time came later, when *Vasa* had broken the surface.

now know that in all probability seven master-carvers were employed to decorate the ship as befitted a king's ship. Of these 'image-carvers' Master Marten signed a receipt for 354 *dalers*, Master Hans received 129 *dalers* and Gert 97 *dalers* 16 *öre*. More modest sums were also paid to Johan Thesson and Petter for the same service. In 1628 the king also took into his employ an 'image-carver' brought in from abroad, a certain Marcus Ledens. Master Marten has been identified, or rather it is probable that he was identical with Marten Rhedtmer, a famous wood-carver who was the creator of the fine pulpit in Jacob church and an organ-front in Storkyrkan.

Many of the motives used in *Vasa*'s ornamentation are astounding and it is not easy to make up one's mind whether the artist concerned was just giving free play to his sense of fun or was depicting something the symbolism of which we do not understand. No doubt, the experts will one day be able to answer that question.

It was a strange procession of lovely mermaids, fierce warriors, dreadful dragons and other queer figures that emerged from the mud around *Vasa*. It must have cost endless time and labour to carve all those figures and groups of figures. A fully sculptured figure-head was found early on and later some double-sided sculptured ornaments. The collection of them ashore included a recumbent figure of a man with fluttering cloak, and a bird with an eel in its beak. There was also a three-foot-high statue of a Roman crowned with laurel trampling a grinning face. Above the face was a scroll on which was the word TIBERIUS. At first the experts were somewhat bewildered by this, being unable to conceive what the Emperor Tiberius could be doing aboard Gustavus Adolphus II's ship; but they have come since to the conclusion that the statue probably symbolized the triumph

A seventeenth-century seaman who was caught under one of the gun-carriages

The remains of another victim of the catastrophe. By the summer of 1961 a good twenty of those who went down with the ship in 1628 had been found

Another of *Vasa*'s guns was found on 6 June 1961, the third

The deep mud and slime inside the ship contained thousands of interesting objects. Here, the archæologists have just found the remains of a musket. All mud and slime was sifted in specially constructed sieves

The King of Sweden, himself an active archæologist, inspecting one of the journals recording finds

The gun-carriages still stand in their places on the lower battery-deck

Archaeologists at work on the lower battery-deck

Work on the lower battery-deck nearing completion

A part of the seventeenth century (lower battery-deck)

Ten thousand litres a minute spurting out of *Vasa*

The chains being fixed on the hydraulic jacks on the pontoon

Vasa looking long and slender as she lies between the two pontoons, *Oden* and *Frigg*. Her stern is nearest the camera. The hydraulic jacks are on the small platforms on the side of the pontoon turned towards *Vasa*. The staging in the middle is where they were originally mounted. The midships shaft is now covered over

The last few yards into the safety of the dry dock were very critical. A wire catching and dislodging a gun-port or a patch could easily have sunk her

of good over evil. Tiberius had a pretty bad reputation as an emperor and his is the ugly face being trampled. A large number of fiercely glaring lions' faces was found. These were fixed on the inside of the gun-ports.

The finds have made it possible to conclude how various parts of *Vasa*'s ornamentation were painted. For example, the inside of the gun-ports were painted red while the lion's face was in all probability gilded and had a red mouth, white teeth and white eye-balls.

The great ship's huge rudder was brought up towards the end of November 1958. It weighs a good three tons, is nearly thirty-four feet long and made of two enormous pieces of oak with a combined width of four feet nine inches. The blade is sixteen inches thick, but its area is comparatively small. The boat must have been steered mainly by manipulating the sails, and the rudder can only have been used for fine adjustment of her course. The head of the rudder probably carried some ornament, a lion's head or something like that, and there was probably ornamentation on the stock as well, but that has not yet been found.

In September 1958, the divers brought up one of *Vasa*'s guns. As we know, numbers of them were salvaged in the seventeenth century, probably fifty-four, but the exact number is not known, so it is impossible to say how many have still to be recovered. This gun was in the sternmost gun-port in the lower battery on the port side. As it was in the way and also threatening to slip out, it was thought best to remove it. It was classified as a short 24-pounder with a calibre of some 14·8 cm. Altogether *Vasa* had carried forty-eight 24-pounders, so their combined weight must have been nearly seventy tons.

Once the gun had been cleaned, it was seen that the

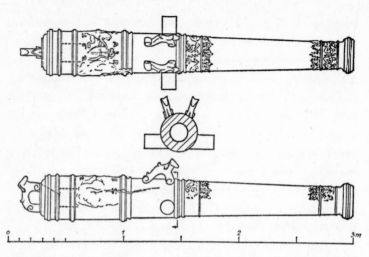

A 24-pounder from *Vasa*, drawn by Captain Sam Svensson of the Museum of Maritime History

rear part of the ornamentation was defective owing to some fault in casting, but the stylized sheaf, emblem of the Vasas, was clearly identifiable. To either side was a so-called dolphin, or handle for lifting the gun, in this case the dolphin being not a dolphin, but a wolf. On the chamber-piece are the letters GARS and the figures 162?, the last figure being illegible. Like most of *Vasa*'s guns, this one was probably made at the gun-foundry at Brunke-bergstorg. The final boring and polishing of these guns was done at the admiralty's own boring-mill and works, which obtained their power from Norrström. A sample of the metal used in the gun has since been analysed, as has a sample from a gun salvaged in 1920 from the *Rik-snyckeln*. The analysis makes it seem probable that the copper used in both guns came from the great Falun mine. It has also been established that, after casting, the guns were heated till they were red-hot in order to toughen them. Judging by the coating of the barrel, *Vasa*'s gun had never been fired.

A sensational find was that of the lion that formed the main motif of the figure-head. This was one of the last finds made before *Vasa* was raised. There is nothing like it of the kind, and it is also thirty years older than the oldest figure-head known hitherto. It is a great lion, couched ready to spring, to have at the enemy, ten feet seven inches long, twenty-five inches wide, and three feet tall. When a hose was turned on it, a glitter of gold appeared among the lion's mane. It may have been the work of Marten Rhedtmer himself.

These finds have told us a lot and have lots more to tell. In time, books will be written about them alone.

10. *Preparations for the Final Lift*

Vasa had come through the stress and strains of her stage-by-stage journey of 1959 with flying colours. This became obvious as soon as divers went down to inspect her in her new resting-place. They found superficial grazes where the lifting-wires had chafed the hull, and some of the bulwark posts had been broken, but there was nothing to indicate that *Vasa* had been subjected to more than she had been able to withstand, and so the committee felt justified in going ahead and planning the next stage.

There was little or no rest for the divers at this stage. Almost as soon as the salvage vessels and pontoons had departed, they were being sent down again, amongst other things to take fresh and more exact measurements of the old ship, and to make a thorough examination of her outside. These new measurements showed that those made in deep water had been amazingly accurate.

Later that autumn, divers were sent down to see what had happened to the hole out of which the old ship had been lifted after lying there for 330 years. Naturally, a good deal of ooze and clay had fallen into it. Some experimental 'digs' were made and these showed that it was going to be perfectly possible to clear up the area, though it might prove a lengthy process. During the fortnight that the divers worked at *Vasa*'s first resting-place, they made a hundred or so interesting finds. Then the weather be-

came too severe and work was stopped at the beginning
of December.

The whole *Vasa* undertaking had now become so large
and complicated that the admiralty suggested to the
government that a special *Vasa* Board should be set up
to assume responsibility for all further activities. This was
done, and in October 1959 the board held its first meeting
under the chairmanship of H.R.H. the Prince of Halland.

May 1960 saw the start of the final preparations.
There was much that still remained to be done, and
Fälting and his divers had to spend many more arduous
hours down with *Vasa*. It was not tunnelling, but quite
different things, that occupied them now. The first and
most important thing to be done was to clear the upper
battery-deck of all the slime, slag, ashes, rubble and old
anchors that had accumulated there over the years. They
had to work carefully even here, however, in order not
to damage any finds that might be lying buried there.
The rest of the work called for men able to carry out
quite advanced joinery under water, for the divers of the
seventeenth century had treated *Vasa* in the most ruth-
less manner during their successful attempts to salve her
valuable guns, and their work of destruction had been
continued down the centuries by the vessels that had
innocently anchored on the old ship, and some of this
had now to be made good. Many were the skippers who
must have cursed and sworn at the unknown object that
robbed them of their good sound anchors. The divers
found twenty-nine of these, all of different sizes and from
different periods, so that it is really surprising that the
old ship had suffered as little as she had. As it was, her
high sterncastle had gone, been demolished, that was
known, and also the fact that the anchor of the ship that
had been forced to anchor on her in fog some time in

1958 had completed the destruction of the after-part. What was lucky was that so many of the carvings fixed to the outside of the ship had dropped off and fallen into the ooze beside the old ship, to lie there and be nicely preserved.

Before the old ship could be brought up, she had to be made as water-tight as possible and so the divers or underwater joiners had to try to fit her with a whole new after-part. This was comparable in size to a small barn, and it had to be built in opaque water. Not only that, but the hull had to be strengthened, so that it could withstand the stresses and strains of breaking the surface. This was done with iron rods which were shackled together in threes and passed through opposite gun-ports on either side, where they were then fixed with nuts to iron girders placed on the outside of the hull. *Vasa* was strengthened thus in four places. Not only that, but all the gun-ports had to be closed and made tight. Another and more difficult job was to search out and fill up all the thousands of holes left by the iron pins and bolts, once used to give the great hull its strength and stability, that had rusted away. Doing this in the opaque waters of Stockholm harbour was a monotonous task and one that called for endless patience. Although the depth was no longer great, visibility was still wretched.

The Eleventh International Congress of Historians was held in Stockholm in the late summer of 1960, and what could have been more natural than to invite the 2,000 attending to a special demonstration of the salvage work being carried out on *Vasa*? Thus, for an hour *Vasa* was the centre of interest of some forty million TV viewers in eight different countries, giving the divers a welcome change in the monotony of their long job.

Two destroyers and a floating crane provided an amphitheatre capable of accommodating some 3,000 spectators. The TV camera whirred, Press photographers clicked feverishly and reporters scribbled away for dear life, while the historians and heralds of the whole world watched the salvage of an old ship's anchor, a gun-carriage and the second gun to be brought up in modern times. The show included a demonstration by a naval captain of a replica of the diving-bell used by Treileben in the seventeenth century. He gave a running commentary in Swedish, English and French during the five minutes he was down, describing how he could not see the old ship though he could feel her. Visibility was only three feet down there and he had to grope his way along the side.

A national collection was now started to obtain funds for the undertaking. A special *Vasa* coin was struck and sold in all branches of the Svenska Handelsbanken as part of a great campaign to obtain funds for *Vasa*. Each coin bought brought with it a share in a *Vasa* lottery.

Work on *Vasa* herself was able to continue right up to Christmas, thanks to the unusual mildness of the winter. Meanwhile, experts were consulted and discussions held on the many points and difficulties that still awaited solution. What still had to be decided was the vital question: could *Vasa* be salved as she was, or would something happen at the last moment to throw a spanner in the works? Dare they work out a timetable? Timetables are not usual in salvage work, where anything can happen, but the eyes of the world were fixed on *Vasa* and particulars of when she was due to be up and visible were impatiently awaited. After some discussion it was decided to aim at all preparations being completed by 4 April 1961, when the salvage fleet was to anchor over

Vasa. The ship herself was to be raised some time between 20 and 27 April.

There was excitement in the air. Sales of the *Vasa* coin increased. A further 50,000 had to be minted. Early in January, the *Vasa* men went back to work, patiently, systematically plugging, strengthening, bracing the old hull. Even the pessimists now began to feel that the old ship was going to be got up—but still there was no certainty. That was what made the whole thing so fascinating.

Despite this uncertainty, the time had now come when they must go ahead with the costly business of preparing a worthy, even if only temporary, home for *Vasa* and the finds. Others who were kept busy were the archæologists. They had to plan all their work without anything to go by, for no such job had ever fallen to archæologists before. They knew little of how *Vasa* would look inside or of what they would find there. Those who had to preserve and conserve had their own problems to solve.

The *Vasa* lottery was drawn at the end of January and, shortly afterwards, Svenska Handelsbanken was able to send the *Vasa* Board a cheque for one million crowns. This was a most welcome addition to the board's budget, for the sum provided by the State was far from sufficient to meet all its needs.

In the middle of March, the Navy sent a number of frogmen and with their help the 6,000 holes left in *Vasa*'s stout oaken sides by iron bolts rusting away were all plugged with wooden pins.

11. *She Breaks the Surface*

The day for the final lift was approaching fast and excitement increased. Souvenir manufacturers and vendors of every description were in full activity. The salvage fleet began to assemble.

The two pontoons, *Oden* and *Frigg*, had for some time been lying alongside Strandvägskajen, one of Stockholm's more fashionable promenades. On 4 April, two of the Neptune Company's salvage vessels, *Atlas* and *Ajax*, arrived and were anchored in place near *Vasa*, where they were joined by *Sleipner*, a lifting-vessel, and the two pontoons. The fleet was completed by the Navy's submarine salvage boat, *Belos*. There were now seventy men under Captain Hedberg's orders. The following day, a Press conference was held on board *Sleipner* at which the representatives of the Press, radio, TV, etc., were told what it was planned to do. It was a grey day with an icy wind blowing across the open deck.

'If all goes as we calculate,' the salvage chief informed the shivering company, '*Vasa* will break the surface for the first time in 333 years some time between 20 and 27 April. It is still too early to say definitely when. Immediately after this, we shall continue work on her, strengthening the hull where necessary, and making it water-tight. The archæologists will be brought in at an early stage to help lighten the ship and, if possible, do away with the list she at present has. A very important

G

part of the work will be that of pumping the water out of her, and this will begin immediately after the lift. As soon as *Vasa* is floating high enough to clear the threshold of the Gustav V dock, it is intended to take her in there. It is calculated that it will be possible to do this some time in the first half of May.

'In dry dock, *Vasa* will be placed on a special concrete pontoon now under construction. This will be the largest of its kind ever built in Sweden. It will be 180 feet long, sixty-eight feet broad, twelve feet high, and will have a lifting-power of 2,000 tons.' (This pontoon was being built at a cost price only, as part of Swedish industry's contribution to the *Vasa* project. Into its construction went 1,000 cubic metres of concrete, 125 tons of reinforcing iron, 10,000 cubic feet of timber and 1,000 square metres of plywood, and much of this was the gift of the suppliers.)

'Once *Vasa* has been bedded down on this pontoon, she will probably never leave it,' the salvage chief went on. 'In other words, it will constitute the floor of the *Vasa* museum of the future, wherever this comes to be. If all goes according to plan and *Vasa* doesn't spring any surprises, we plan to hold a special *Vasa* Day on 17 June, when *Vasa* on her pontoon will be towed to a site now being prepared, where she is to be exhibited for the time being.'

The two pontoons, *Oden* and *Frigg*, now to be used a second time in *Vasa*'s salvage, were built in the 1890s to salve a Russian battleship that had sunk in the Gulf of Finland. They had been modernized several times since. They were equipped with big hydraulic lifting-jacks, whose tall stands were erected over a long well running from fore to aft down the midship line. When the jacks are used, simple nine-inch wires are placed under the vessel to be raised and up through the well between the two halves of the pontoon. When this method is used, however, the wreck concerned can only be lifted as far as the bottom of the pontoons. In salving *Vasa*, it was felt best to aim straight away at getting her so far up that a start could be made on pumping the water out of her, while she still hung in the relative security of her wires. To make this possible the Neptune Company had decided to move the jacks to the sides of the two pontoons, which would enable them to lift the ship in one operation. The pontoons, each of which could lift some 1,200 tons, while *Vasa* now weighed some 600 tons, were considered to have enough displacement in reserve to provide the necessary trim to overcome this oblique load.

The day after the Press conference, *Oden* and *Frigg* were filled with water and sunk in place. Then the six-inch wires that had been used when *Vasa* was first raised and moved in 1959, and which still lay in place under her, were attached to the pontoons, the water was pumped out of the pontoons and *Vasa* raised some thirteen feet. When divers went down to see that all was well, they found that *Vasa* had slipped in her wires. How or when this had happend no one knew. It probably happened in 1959; but the fact remained that the stern-most pair of wires that ought to have been some 110 feet from the stern was now only eighty feet from it, which meant that far too much of the ship was hanging unsupported. Naturally, they did not dare risk lifting *Vasa* in that position. She could easily have broken in two. There was nothing for it, but to lower her on to the bottom again and let the divers dredge round the stern-part till they could pass a fresh pair of wires under her nearer the stern.

It was not a good beginning, and it looked as though the timetable was already in danger. The period for the final lift was only a fortnight away.

It was no easy matter getting the new wires in place, but the divers managed it quickly and well. It proved, however, that a new pair of wires was not going to be enough if they were to feel really safe. Further support was needed for the after-part. As it happened, rubber pontoons with a combined lifting-power of twenty tons had been obtained—as a precaution—early on in the proceedings, and these were now brought into use and placed at the stern to give it extra support. In a few days all was ready for a fresh lift, and it was not long then before *Vasa* was again hanging in her wires between the two pontoons. The time had now come when the divers would be able to see *Vasa*'s bottom for the first time. It was realized that in all probability she would be holed, but how extensive would the damage be? Big gaping holes impossible to patch? Or not so bad? There was no knowing.

It was an exciting bottom-inspection and one that was not entirely free from risk. A big wake set up by a careless boat could all too easily have set *Vasa* swinging in her wires and such motion could crush and kill the divers. Repeated warnings had been issued and every day the wireless exhorted all taking boats into the area to show care and consideration—and so most people did.

A couple of naval divers were the first to slip under *Vasa*. Their initial report sounded promising. The bottom looked fine. The wires that had borne the great ship on her eighteen-stage journey the year before had left scarcely any marks on her great keel. The bottom planks were as hard as stone.

While the work of making the hull tight continued,

they began changing the wires. The fact that they were going to use hydraulic jacks in the next lift meant that the old six-inch wires had to be replaced by the thicker wires that were coupled to the lifting-chains of the jacks, which look like huge bicycle chains.

Step by step the work progressed, sometimes smoothly, sometimes with minor mishaps that quickness of wit and initiative soon rendered harmless. Soon they had caught up with the timetable. The lost time had been made up. Captain Gedberg drove his men to the utmost. Work began at five o'clock each morning and continued without interruption till seven or eight in the evening, seven days a week. It was a particularly lovely spring and fine weather favoured the work.

By 14 April it seemed that things were far enough advanced for it to be possible to fix the day of the final lift: Monday, 24 April. In actual fact the coupling of the nine-inch wires to the jack-chains proved easier than had been expected and it was 17 April when *Vasa* rose from the bottom for the last time. The fourteen jacks were manned early in the morning—two men to each—and with the utmost caution, inch by inch, they drew up the chains, while attentive eyes watched the manometers that were fitted to each jack. A good 220 tons was now resting on the port jacks and, as *Vasa*'s weight was now reckoned to have been reduced to just over 400 tons, that meant that she still had a list. The loss of weight was due to the divers' clearing operations: one gun, some tons of stone, many cubic yards of ooze and slime, slag and ashes, plus a number of loose bits of water-logged oak, weigh more than a little. As the ship was lifted, the pontoons had to be trimmed by pumping in water to prevent them heeling over too far towards *Vasa*. The ship's upward journey was accomplished safely and that evening she was hanging securely on the jacks with her upper part only a few feet under water.

Public interest was now intense. The *Vasa* Board's telephones never stopped ringing and people came down to Skeppsholm and Kastellholm in such numbers that the police had to close the bridge to wheeled traffic. Skeppsholm and Kastellholm had been one of the Swedish Navy's main bases for close on 300 years, and it was only recently, after the main part of the Stockholm base had been moved out to the archipelago, that the two little islands had been opened to the public.

The great day dawned, Monday, 24 April, the day of *Vasa*'s resurrection, a day of brilliant sunshine, excitement and, perhaps, a little anxiety. Work on the final preparations began at five o'clock. Some 300 Swedish and foreign reporters had applied for tickets, and the first of these began to arrive shortly afterwards. The naval launches lay ready to start the shuttle-service that was to fetch the board's own guests. The harbour police boats kept circling round seeing that all water-traffic behaved itself. At eight o'clock the flags went up. Astern of *Vasa* lay *Lodbrok*, a big floating-crane, now a roomy grandstand for this very special occasion, Some of the steamers of the archipelago had been anchored alongside to provide extra space.

The first of the guests began to arrive at eight o'clock. The Navy's own band provided music and whatever was going on was reported at intervals through loudspeakers. Every helicopter in Stockholm had been chartered and an aerial traffic-control station had been set up on *Belos* to prevent the noise of planes overhead drowning the orders given to the salvage men, who were now standing by at the hydraulic jacks. At nine o'clock the jacks began to work and at three minutes past nine a piece of black seventeenth-century oak suddenly broke through the surface of the brown water. This was all that remained of the old sterncastle. Slowly, infinitely slowly, the line of the bulwark-posts began to rise out of the water. By ten o'clock there was still more to be seen. By eleven, the fore-part was emerging, and all the while the jacks worked on and the pontoons were trimmed. *Vasa* was coming up at the rate of eighteen inches an hour. The people on *Lodbrok* could now see the outline of the deck. Then a couple of wooden figures of warriors became visible on the fore-deck. In them were the block-slits through which the sheet and tack for the foresail and foretopsail used to run.

It was two o'clock or so before the line of the deck reached the surface. Anders Franzén, *Vasa's* re-discoverer, and Fälting, who had headed the team of divers, prepared to step aboard and take possession of the ship. First, they rowed across her deck in a plastic dinghy, then they stepped aboard on to a beam in the after-part, shook hands and sacrificed a coin to the spirit of *Vasa*.

As far as the public was concerned, that concluded the day's proceedings, but the salvage men still had several hours' work ahead of them to get all ready for the morrow's move into shallower water.

Early the next morning, the tugs arrived and slowly the two pontoons and *Vasa* were towed 220 yards nearer the shore. The whole business took about an hour, at the end of which *Vasa* was anchored with her fore-part some thirteen feet off the bottom in thirty-two feet of water and her after-part just touching in thirty-nine feet.

The pumpers and archæologists were anxious to start work, but, before they could begin, *Vasa* had to be raised

eighteen inches. The sun blazed down and those in charge
of preserving her and her timbers gazed anxiously at bulwark-posts, deck-beams and knees. The most delicate of
the exposed bits had to be put in plastic covers as quickly
as possible, and some means of sprinkling the whole with
water must be devised to prevent the timbers drying out
too quickly.

As soon as the hydraulic jacks had raised *Vasa* the
necessary distance, they were able to begin pumping the
water out of her. Transportable pumps were standing
ready on *Oden*'s deck. Although they had a capacity of
ten tons a minute, they weighed only ten hundredweight
each. This pumping was a delicate job that called for
extreme care. It had to be exactly synchronized with the
raising of the ship. The level of the water inside the ship
must never be allowed to rise higher than that of the
water outside, otherwise the ship's side would be exposed
to abnormal strain in the form of outward pressure from
within. The iron rods that had been passed right through
the ship in four places would probably prevent a catastrophe, but having got so far, they dare not take any
risks. Also, as *Vasa* rose, the weight of water in her
decreased; the pontoons had to be continually trimmed
to ensure that she still had plenty of support from the
lifting-wires. Two pumping-shafts had been prepared,
one forward and one aft, and into these the Flygt pumps
were now lowered; soon 4,500 gallons of water a minute
were pouring out from the old ship, enough to fill 150
bath-tubs every minute. It was while preparing these
pump-shafts that they found one of *Vasa*'s own wooden
pumps. Originally caulked with pitch, it was still water-
tight. It had a capacity of between 4·4 and almost
eleven gallons a minute, depending on the distance of
travel and the number of men on the levers. As soon as

Vasa sailing into the dock on her own keel. In the foreground is the big generator that provided current for the pumps, which were kept working all the time as *Vasa* was still leaking badly

The big *Vasa* pontoon being docked in Stockholm after its voyage from Gävle

Owing to the low level of the water and *Vasa*'s unexpectedly great draught, an extra lifting operation had to be performed to get her up on to the concrete pontoon. One of the lifting pontoons is on her port side. She is being positioned for placing on the grooved block on the pontoon

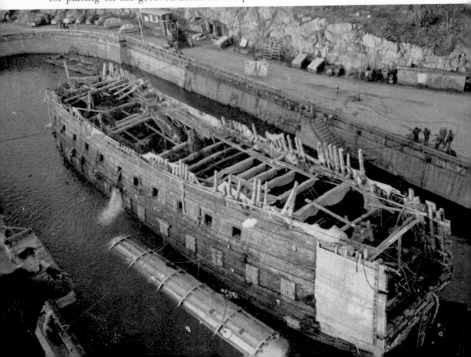

Vasa high and dry. At her stern can be seen three of the rubber pontoons used to give her extra support. Note the elegant stern-part the divers carpentered for her under water

This is what a seven-teenth-century Swedish sailor looked like. The house that is to prevent *Vasa* from drying out too quickly is beginning to take shape. The concrete arches visible over her stern weigh eighteen tons a piece

Vasa from starboard

Vasa cleared for taking out. In the foreground is a cannon, removed on 6 June 1961, along with two of the nearly thirty anchors found in her.

Out of dock once more. In July *Vasa* was towed out for further archaeological excavation. Even while being towed, the sprinklers were kept going to prevent her drying out

Model of the pro-
visional exhibition
buildings, where *Vasa*
will be in her own
specially shaped house

pumping began, the divers had to get busy again. *Vasa* was leaking badly through innumerable tiny holes and cracks, and divers and frogmen now set about finding these—no easy task—and plugging them with sawdust, tallow and rags, wooden wedges and pins. Then it was discovered that one of the covers put over a gun-port had been dislodged by the lifting-wires and through the resulting gap more water was streaming in than the pumps could pump out. By early afternoon, however, the divers had done their job and the pumps had got the upper hand. That evening, both fore- and after-part of the old ship were six feet above water, and the great beams that had borne the upper deck were also above the surface. Sixteen of these were still in place, the other twelve having been torn loose over the centuries by ships' anchors that had lodged in them.

While the pumpers were pumping and the divers plugging and filling, the archæologists had been waiting impatiently. The chief archæologist, Lundström, had mustered a team of students from Stockholm University, all of whom had done archæological or ethnological fieldwork. One look into *Vasa*'s mud-filled interior was enough to show them what awaited them, but fortunately it was no more than what they had imagined and they were equipped to deal with it. They had been innoculated against every sort of infectious disease, and they were clad from top to toe in rubber and wore steel helmets. The slime was heavy and evil-smelling and they found it hard work. The ship hung heavily in the after-wires and the salvage people kept urging them to get on with it and get the stern lightened.

During the Thursday, the pump's advantage over the incoming water increased and slowly but surely *Vasa* rose. As the hours passed, more of the old ship's real

95

shape became visible, so that she no longer looked like a worn-out coal-lighter covered with slime. The archæ- ologists were doing a twelve-hour day and their Thurs- day's harvest was a good two tons of assorted deck-beams and knees of oak, unidentifiable bits of timber, some heavy, some light; each piece was registered and photo- graphed and put to soak in one of the scores of ordinary baths that stood in lines on a couple of pontoons moored astern of *Vasa*. Larger bits of the hull were wrapped up in plastic and tarpaulin. Every object was given a num- bered label and the main facts about it noted in a special journal. The place where each was found was also recorded.

In the after-part, where *Vasa*'s commander, Captain Söfring Hansson had had his quarters, the scene was like a gold-diggers' camp. Once the more bulky and heavier objects had been removed, the archæologists set to work with specially designed pans washing for what to them was as good as gold. They struck reasonably lucky: a small casket containing some lovely little pewter bottles, a unique carving, some music-playing angels bearing obvious traces of gilding, etc.

The pumping proved most successful, but, as the water sank inside, it left unexpected quantities of slime. On the upper battery-deck the slime lay fifteen inches thick. On the lower battery-deck and the hawser-deck every- thing was buried in three feet of slime and ooze. The whole bilge proved to be full of the same devilish, bubbling, witches' brew, which hid treacherous holes in the deck above and made walking an adventure. Every- where in the slime lay objects of every kind. Most of this vast quantity of slime had to pass through the archæologists' sieves, before their work was complete.

Meanwhile, *Vasa*'s own pontoon had been completed

and launched and was now due to reach Stockholm. A bed of gravel had been prepared for it in the dry dock, where they were now busy preparing for *Vasa*. Early on 29 April, the pontoon arrived and was manœuvred into the dry dock with about three feet to spare on either side. The dock gates were closed and water pumped in. The keel block on which *Vasa* was to stand was rigged and the supports checked. A few days later it was possible to fill the pontoon with water, after which the dock gates were opened and the water poured in, while the future museum floor remained on its gravel bed.

All was now ready to receive *Vasa*, the unique ship.

Vasa would not rise as far as was wanted. Archæologists and salvage and pump experts laboured to help her, but she was still too deep in the water to clear the threshold of the dry dock. The clearance there was some thirty-one feet and, though she was likely to be able to manage that in reasonable time, the real difficulty was that she had to get up on to the special pontoon that was to be her permanent stand, and as this was thirteen feet high, she must not be drawing more than eighteen feet or so of water if she was to mount it. The days passed and the salvage people began to grow a little impatient. The old ship seemed to be making fools of them. The archæologists forced the pace as best they could, sometimes even compromising with their academic conscience in order to answer the call for speed.

No one had anticipated finding so much mud and slime inside the ship. There was an enormous amount of it, and it made everybody's work far more complicated. It even proved necessary to install a special dredging-pump, for which a pump-shaft was made amidships. The pump used was a model designed for clearing choked-up lakes. It sucked eight tons of slime a minute out of the old ship. Its inlet pipe was covered with a piece of fine-meshed netting to protect any objects of interest that might be lying down near the keel.

It was a real ding-dong struggle. Sometimes the water that seeped and poured in got the upper hand and the old ship sank a few inches, even a foot lower, in the water; at other times the pumps proved superior and *Vasa*'s oaken sides again rose a few inches. Success still hung in the balance and for a few exciting days the salvage people were unwilling to express a definite opinion. Like all sailors they were reluctant to challenge fate by inopportune optimism. They had too much respect for supernatural powers for that. Each new step was discussed in advance and all the things that might happen were anticipated, and measures taken to guard against unpleasant surprises. Fortunately, they were so successful in this that there were none.

The fine weather held. Day after day the sun shone down out of a cloudless sky. The breeze was light and warm. Everybody delighted in the glorious weather—except the *Vasa* people who watched with anxious faces how deck-beams, rail-posts and the ship's sides began to dry out far too quickly in the hot sunshine. The most sensitive parts were already covered with plastic and were sprinkled with water regularly, but the conservation experts wanted everything kept drenched. That, however, just had to wait. Instead, they designed a system of sprinklers that kept the whole ship damp.

The archæologists really had a hard time of it, slipping and slithering in revolting, evil-smelling slime, crawling on hands and knees through narrow holes, sweating in their tight-fitting rubber-suits, stumbling over pipes and hoses, and always they had to move with the utmost caution, because anywhere there might be a treacherous hole in the deck concealed by the layer of mud. Now—almost the last straw—they had to work in the perpetual drizzle of the sprinklers. But nothing damped their enthusiasm and the heaps of finds they had dug out grew quickly under the tarpaulins on the collecting site and in the long row of baths.

Then the pump people really got the situation under control, and slowly but surely *Vasa* rose out of the brown waters of the harbour. The pumps worked day and night and slime-blackened water ran in mighty streams down the ship's sides. Then came the time when the old ship was really afloat, when she moved as the wash of a passing motor-boat reached her. It was an ungainly, awkward movement, but still a sign of life. Shortly after this, *Vasa* was floating high enough to be taken into the dry dock, although she was still lying too deep for her to be able to get on to her pontoon. It was not only the water and the slime in her weighing her down; the oaken timbers of her sides and her stout beams were sodden and heavy with water, so heavy that she just could not be made to rise high enough by pumping alone. More radical measures were called for, especially as the salvage craft were needed for other work and could not dance attendance on *Vasa* for ever. Could the archæologists get a move on? No, they could not. They were already working more than twelve hours a day, and from the scientific and academic point of view to have hurried their excavation of this unique site would have been utterly reprehensible. Some other solution had to be devised.

And it was. Instead of docking *Vasa* straightaway on her pontoon, it was decided to take the process in two stages. Fortunately, the dry dock was so large that *Vasa* could be set on its floor astern of the pontoon. Once she was there, the archæologists should be able to work more effectively than out in the waters of the harbour.

And so, on Thursday, 4 May, *Vasa* was towed into her dry dock. But before she could be moved, her list had to be corrected as far as possible, and this was done by placing ten tons of ballast on the starboard upper battery-deck. Tugs were ordered and word was sent that the floating-crane, *Lodbrok*, would be needed to move the big mooring-buoys. She was wanted for twelve o'clock, but twelve o'clock came and there was no sign of her familiar silhouette. Then, at last she appeared. It transpired that, when word came that she was needed to help, her services were already bespoken to place a 6,000 h.p. diesel engine in a steamer, and this had proved a slightly longer job than had been anticipated; as a result, she was late in reaching her rendezvous.

The weather was ideal. It was a calm sunny day. Just before one o'clock the tugs began to move and the little armada set out. First, the ship had to be turned right round—no easy task in that narrow channel—then, her squat fore-part pointing in the right direction, she moved off at two knots heading for the dry dock. The floating-crane had already put out the two buoys that the salvage vessels needed to get the correct alignment for the dock gates. Now came the most exciting moment of all. The lifting pontoons that had been on either side of *Vasa* the whole time could not go into the dry dock with her, so the hawsers had to be cast off and the old ship left to manage the last stretch on her own. The only real danger here was that, in casting off the wires, one of them might have dislodged one of the water-tight covers over the gun-ports, and then *Vasa* would have gone down despite the pumps that were still working away in her. For a moment it looked as though this was exactly what was going to happen, for one of the after-wires did catch on something on *Vasa*'s bottom, and a couple of frogmen had to be sent down to deal with the situation. Fortunately, it was nothing serious. Then the lifting-wire of the dock's big crane was attached to *Vasa* and, freed of her pontoons and salvage vessels, she glided with a slight list over the threshold and into the safe refuge of the dry dock.

Captain Hedberg heaved a sigh of relief and lit a cigar. His job was accomplished. He had done his part. The rest was up to the dockyard people.

12. *In Dry Dock at Last*

A new epoch began when the dock gates closed behind *Vasa*. Gone was the risk that she might go to the bottom again; but instead other dangers threatened. No one knew for sure how the old ship's hull would react to sunlight and heat; nor even what would happen when she was laid high and dry: would the hull stand up to the stresses and strains that would be put upon her? How could she best be supported and shored up to prevent the timbers cracking or the hull settling? Would the old ship even stand being laid high and dry with all that ballast in her belly? And anyway how much ballast was there? How could it be got out quickly?

There were plenty of problems to be solved, but not the time to tackle them quietly and peacefully, for the programme was that *Vasa* should remain in the dry dock for about six weeks, after which time she would have to make way for the government ice-breakers that had to be got ready for the winter. This meant that the work had to be pressed forward relentlessly, for there was a great deal to be done, before *Vasa*, on her big concrete pontoon, could be towed to the mooring-place intended for her opposite Skeppsholm. Not only was there this wealth of problems, but as often as not the technicians, the archæologists and those in charge of the work of conservation had diametrically opposed ideas as to how they could best be solved. Endless meetings and discussions were held, and as a rule the solution arrived at was in the nature of a compromise.

Vasa's first few days in dry dock were ones of real excitement. Slowly and carefully the water was pumped out of the dock, while *Vasa* was propped at the sides and shored up from underneath. More and more of the stout oak hull became visible. One could scarcely say that the old ship was a beautiful sight; perhaps the sailor or ship-builder of today would say that she never had been, but certainly the 333 years she had spent at the bottom of the sea had left their mark on her. On the other hand, they did not seem to have had much effect on her stout oaken hull. There are without doubt wooden boats built at the beginning of this century, whose bottoms are in much worse shape than *Vasa*'s. Her main deck had been torn off by Treileben and his men, but the remaining deck-beams give a good idea of how she must have looked. Above the line of the deck rise the frame-timbers and bulwark-stanchions, some whole, others broken off. The high sterncastle, in which the officers once lived, had disappeared altogether.

Vasa's hull is undoubtedly impressive. Her unusually ample fore-part gives an impression of solid strength, while her broad bows show that she was no greyhound of the seas. In all probability, her ability to manœuvre was not of the best, either. Her sides, black and glistening with moisture, rose like the walls of a house when you saw them from the bottom of the dock, and the whole spirit of the seventeenth century poured from the two rows of rectangular gun-ports. The water-line was roughly four feet below the lower line of these gun-ports and one did not need to be a naval architect to see why *Vasa*'s maiden voyage had been so short and dramatic. Tall rigging, enormous superstructure, heavy armament

H

and a wealth of carving and ornamentation, mostly placed high up, made all ships of those days a bit top-heavy. Seen from astern, the part of the old ship below the water-line was almost graceful. The jagged remains of the sterncastle ended almost fifty-five feet above her keel. The rudder itself had been salvaged long ago. It was more than thirty-two feet high and weighed a good three tons. Everything to do with *Vasa* is big, massive and heavy, and feet and inches seem inadequate to give a true impression of her dimensions. Just to say that she is 156 feet long and has a beam of thirty-nine feet at her broadest point seems to tell so little. It would be better if one could reckon out how many giant oak trees had gone into the building of her massive frame.

So the days passed and the archæologists sweated blood to try to keep up with the timetable. The crane hoisted out basket upon basket of fresh finds and deposited them on the quay: small pieces of wood and big seaman's-chests, parts of the rigging, carvings, cannon-balls and much besides. They were exciting days for those in charge of conservation. The soaking baths they had prepared were soon filled and they hastily had to build others to accommodate the finds that were continually being made.

On 6 June, Sweden's national day, the king presented the *Vasa* team with a replica of the flag the old ship had flown on her maiden voyage. It was over twenty feet long and thirteen feet deep; the colours, dark indigo blue and orange yellow, considerably richer than those of the present Swedish flag, were copied from an old Swedish flag preserved in Amsterdam. This was the king's first visit to his warship. The king for whom she was built never went aboard her. That was left to his successor, Gustaf Adolf VI, who now spent more than two hours in her, wearing one of the archæologist's work-

ing suits, going everywhere, seeing everything and study-
ing the finds. (The King of Sweden is himself an amateur
archæologist of considerable experience.)

The immediate problem and the one that overshadowed
everything else was that of getting *Vasa* up on to her
concrete pontoon. Her ballast was right at the bottom in
the bilge and difficult to get at. Hard as they worked, the
archæologists were not getting out nearly as much of the
enormous quantity of mud and ooze deposited inside the
old ship, as had been expected, and *Vasa* was still too
heavy and would have too big a draught when the dock
was filled again. Not only that, but latterly the level of
the water in Stockholm harbour has been abnormally
low. Something had to be done, if the timetable was not
to be dislocated too seriously.

Captain Hedberg, whose task had been thought completed when he delivered *Vasa* safely into dry dock, was
called back to undertake a miniature lifting operation, it
being necessary now to raise *Vasa* inside the dry dock
itself. This entailed using smaller pontoons that would
fit in alongside her in the dock. So, soon the Neptune
Company's people were again busy about the old ship,
coupling together four cylindrical pontoons with a lifting
force of a hundred tons apiece and getting everything
ready for the last lift of all. The water was still unusually
low, so low that even the pontoons would not be able to
lift the old ship high enough to get her on to her floor.
Then one evening the water suddenly rose, at the same
time as the meteorologists sent warning of approaching
changes that would cause it to sink again soon. It was an
opportunity that had to be seized quickly. Slowly the dock
was filled and it was not long before *Vasa* was afloat again.
Slowly and carefully she was hauled across over her pontoon, the future floor of the *Vasa* Museum. It was a pre-

cision job. The margin was tiny. In fact, *Vasa* cleared the block in which her keel was to rest with less than half an inch to spare at the stern. Everyone heaved sighs of relief when at last she was in place and could be lowered on to the block.

The fact that it had been so difficult to get *Vasa* up on to her pontoon could also be an indication that she was considerably heavier than had originally been calculated. This meant that it was a matter of urgency to lighten the hull of its burden of mud and ballast. It was tough, sticky mud and to deal with it they were now forced to use the sluice-and-suck method, which involved cautiously pumping large quantities of water into the hull. This water loosened the mud in the bilge and the resultant 'soup' could then be pumped out. Once the layer of mud and slime had been sufficiently reduced to get at the ballast, it became possible to use an elevator to take out the stones of which this consisted.

As we know, the original estimate had been that *Vasa* must have been carrying about 400 tons of ballast, and it was thus a considerable surprise when it gradually became apparent that she did not have more than 120 tons of stone in her bilge.

The pumping out of the muddy water, digging out the stones, and emptying them out of the old ship took a lot of time, and when 17 June came *Vasa* was far from ready to leave the dry dock, which she then had to share with *Ymer*, the ice-breaker. It was not till 26 July that *Vasa* could be taken out of dry dock.

13. *The Finds*

The finds made by the archæologists in the vast masses of slime and mud inside the old ship were a strange mixture. There were seemingly worthless little bits of wood, interesting tools and utensils, and carvings that set one's imagination working. It is still impossible to give anything like a comprehensive list of what was found. *Vasa* was handsomely ornamented, to say the least of it, and many of the carvings are beautiful, but they do not have such a great deal to tell us. What is of most interest is how things looked behind this gorgeous façade. Did what was inside correspond in any way to the magnificence of the ship's exterior? Apparently, far from it! The conditions in which seamen and naval ratings lived in those days were wretched in the extreme. Pay was bad and usually in arrears, the food was wretched, clothing elementary, discipline iron-hard and the cruellest punishments were meted out for even the slightest misdemeanour. Flogging, mutilation and keel-hauling were nothing unusual in the warships of those days. A striking number of drinking vessels made of wood and pewter, plus a number of beer kegs, have been found, evidence that beer was as big an ingredient in the diet of the seventeenth-century sailor as of the landlubber. The beer ration in those days was indeed enormous, but it must have taken a good deal of liquid to wash down the salt, dry and often rancid fare that the sailor was given.

According to the Navy Laws of 1535, the beer ration was laid down at one barrel, or about thirty gallons, per twenty-four hours for every forty men. But six pints for twenty-four hours were not considered enough, and in 1559 the ration was increased, and after then thirty men shared the barrel. However, those serving in His Majesty's ships seemed to become thirstier and thirstier, and by the middle of the seventeenth century it was considered that a seaman ought to have at least three stoups (fourteen pints) a day, when at sea. The year *Vasa* went down (1628), Gustavus Adolphus II issued instructions that the fleet was to be supplied with sufficient bread and beer 'so that the crews might have more or less adequate sustenance and not be constrained to drink salt water which in past years has been the cause of so many falling sick and losing their lives to the great detriment and noticeable loss of His Majesty and His Realm'. This naval beer was brewed in three strengths: 'master's' beer for the captains and masters, 'bailiff's' beer for the other officers and mates, and table-beer for the ratings. With a ration of this size, the Swedish fleet at that time was consuming some 120,000 gallons of beer a year.

The remains of some twenty of the unhappy wretches who went down with *Vasa* have been found, some crushed under a gun-carriage, others trapped in some cavity, others again just lying on deck. Many parts of the skeletons are well preserved, and they and the skulls with their grinning white rows of teeth will have interesting information to impart.

The lower down the archæologists penetrated, the more exciting did their work become. The atmosphere on the lower battery-deck was truly that of the seventeenth century, and there one scarcely spoke above a whisper, afraid to shatter the silence that the massive deck-timbers above one's head seem to impose. On the planks of the deck itself, the knees and frame-timbers, the marks of the shipwrights' axes were still evident, and although the divers of the seventeenth century had removed the guns, the gun-carriages stood in their proper places. A number of them still had their lashings and ties intact. A store of ramrods and powder-scoops was found, as also was a quantity of the crew's personal effects. Beside one of the gun-carriages lay a complete skeleton, on which fragments of clothing still remained and also a pair of shoes in quite good condition.

From the lower battery-deck, the archæologists went straight to the bilge, because it was essential to get the ballast uncovered and out of the ship as soon as possible. It was there, in the bilge, that they found the ship's anchor hawser, amongst other things. This was some 1,300 feet long and six inches in diameter. Dry, it must have weighed somewhere in the region of two and a half tons. A modern hawser of this size made by machinery would cost about £1,700. In the storage space a number of pickling vessels were found containing the bones of pigs and cattle. Kegs of musket-balls were also found there and a large number of round 24-pounder shot. Round shot, chain-shot, scissor-shot, and peak-shot were also found in the ammunition store. Another interesting find was that of the ship's carpenter's tool-box, which contained, amongst numbers of other things, a wooden bit-brace, axe-hafts, a breast-drill and planes, knife-handles, a whetstone and a winder. Other finds included various domestic articles such as plates made of wood and pewter, pottery bowls, wooden kegs, jugs and earthenware jars, pewter bottles, wooden spoons, etc. Among the more curious objects are parts of a table-clock, a small fire-dish presumably for preparing food, a spiggott, with a tap shaped like a cock, and a wooden pocket sun-dial; a number of small personal possessions like combs, buttons, hooks and eyes, a breast-pin and a signet ring of twenty-three carat gold; and there is also a box containing a lock of hair.

One of the great moments was when the first seaman's chest to be found was opened. It was a devout little gathering that witnessed this unique event. It was a good stout chest made of oak. On top lay a three-cornered hat in an excellent state of preservation; beside it was a little chip-box that proved to contain a sewing-ring, a ball of thread and some pieces of cloth. Under the hat was an empty brandy or spirits keg that would hold some three and a half pints, a pair of slippers, a pair of shoes and a wooden shoe-last, presumably used as a model when ordering or making new shoes. At the bottom of the chest was a pair of gloves in good condition and a purse containing coins. The lock of the chest had rusted away and was broken, and a good deal of mud had got in. Fragments of material were found in it on the bottom. The chip-box bore a distinct house-mark, which is the same as that used by the ancestors of a Gotland family.

The coins in the purse are some of the 3,500 that have been found in various parts of the ship. These include a quantity of one-*öre* pieces minted in Dalarna. (In 1628 a chicken cost six *öre* and a sheep twenty-four.) But the ship's cash-box has not yet been found.

The galley or ship's kitchen was right down in the bilge. It is a rectangular space with brick walls and, as far as can be judged, it was there that all the food for the crew was prepared in large pots over an open fire.

The old ship had two pumps, both still in good condition. One consisted of the trunk of an alder tree, twenty-six feet long, which had been hollowed out. To prevent it cracking or splitting the bark had been left on it, and it is still there today. The second pump was a double-action one, and its tube was made of lead.

From 25 April to 29 September the archæologists removed 14,000 objects out of *Vasa*, many of them being multiple ones, since coins, for example, were recorded under one number. Previously, the divers had brought up some 4,000 objects, so that the total is well in excess of 20,000, and there are undoubtedly many more yet to be recovered from the mud in and near where *Vasa* lay.

14. *The Conservation of Finds*

The task of preserving and conserving all these finds is one of the utmost interest and also difficulty. In many cases those in charge of this task are working largely in the dark, and new methods and techniques have had to be devised.

Water, ooze and mud have a certain preservative effect on organic matter, and though during their long centuries in the water *Vasa*'s timbers have changed in appearance, on the whole they have stood up to everything remarkably well.

The wood in *Vasa* now had a soft outer layer, which varies in depth according to kind. On the deal so far found, for example, it is only a few millimetres thick. Below this soft layer, the wood tissue has suffered considerably less damage and its chemical composition is pretty well that of normal wood, but the soft outer layer has undergone a considerable chemical change. Unless the tissue of this soft layer were reinforced, there would have been a likelihood of it dropping or flaking off during the process of drying. Thus, the immediate concern of the preservers was to protect the timbers against the attack of fungi, which exposure to the air would most probably bring, reinforce the tissue of the wood, and as far as possible reduce the damage likely to be caused by the process of drying with its risk of splitting and warping. For the first, they have been using natriumpentachlorphenolate, while to reinforce the tissue and reduce the dangers of drying, polyethyleneglycol is used. The procedure is gradually to replace the water, or most of it, in the timber with polyethyleneglycol, which stabilizes the dimensions of the wood by penetrating and remaining in the cell-tissue, thus preventing shrinkage. As the walls of the cells are badly damaged, the polyethyleneglycol also acts as a reinforcement, for it gradually congeals into a firm mass which cannot be volatilized or destroyed. Where the larger objects of wood are concerned, it has been necessary first to impregnate them with natriumpentachlorphenolate under pressure in order to protect them against the attack of fungi, before starting on the slower process of replacing the water by polyethyleneglycol.

The more precious objects are treated in a bath, which initially contains a thirty-per-cent solution of polyethyleneglycol. As there is a risk of the wood being attacked by micro-organisms during the process of preservation, it has either to be disinfected beforehand or a suitable disinfectant added to the solution. The length of time each object is kept in the bath depends on its size, the kind of wood, etc. During treatment, the concentration of polyethyleneglycol in the bath is gradually increased by slowly raising the temperature from 20°C. up to 70°C., causing the water to evaporate gradually. The level of liquid is maintained by adding more of the thirty-per-cent solution. When much of the water has evaporated, the temperature has to be raised to just over the point of fusion. After a few days, the smallest objects can be removed and the degree of preservation checked. The larger objects, naturally, have to stay considerably longer in the concentrated solution.

Another method is to move objects from one bath to

another, the solution in each bath being more concentrated than in the one before. When this method is used, it is done in six or eight stages, the objects remaining some weeks in each bath. The great difficulty here is that it is not easy to tell when the objects are ready to be moved to the next bath; thus the tendency is to leave them longer than is necessary, especially as this in no way harms them.

When an object is considered ready and is removed from its bath, it is subjected to radiant heat and all superfluous polyethyleneglycol removed. Its surfaces are then washed with spirit solution and the process is complete.

The main reason why *Vasa* is in such good condition is that there are no ship-worms in the Baltic and thus none in Stockholm harbour. Other favourable factors have been the relatively low temperature of the water and the fact that it is so turbid that short-wave light has not reached the wreck. The mud has also had a preservative effect.

The objects recovered are made of an enormous variety of materials: iron, bronze, pewter, silver, bone, leather, pottery, lead, horn, ivory, tortoise-shell, amber, paper, foodstuffs, medicines, etc. Some have had to be treated immediately, others could safely wait if kept in water in a dark, cool place, while others such as glazed pottery required no attention. Unglazed pottery does require treatment. The most difficult to deal with are paper and leather, but silver is by no means easy since there is sulphuretted hydrogen in the ooze on the bottom and this can cause considerable changes in it.

To illustrate how a find is dealt with, let us follow the pewter box that was found to contain butter. First, it was photographed, then the butter was removed and put in a refrigerator. A small quantity of the butter was then

114

sent to be analysed. The box itself was badly corroded and attacked by pewter-pest, so that to have begun work on it without knowing its original shape might have caused damage to delicate parts; therefore, the next step was to take X-ray pictures in two projections, which showed exactly where the so-called pewter-pest had grown out and altered the shape of the outline with its wart-like bubbles. Some objects of pewter or tin can be so badly attacked as to be impossible to save, for tin can occur in two states: as a silvery-white material, or as a grey powder. It turns into the latter if kept for a long period in a temperature below 13°C.

Gold is the material that gives the preservers least work, but even glass can be attacked by glass-sickness. However, glass was very expensive and rare in Sweden in the seventeenth century and so far no glass objects have been found in *Vasa*. Bronze can be troublesome and cast-iron has a tendency to turn to powder, as has happened with some of the cannon-balls.

Vasa is now in her own house so that the humidity of the atmosphere there and the temperature can be kept constant as desired; thus most of the initial dangers have now been overcome.

15. *Why did Vasa Capsize?*

Why did *Vasa*'s tragedy occur? Was she faultily built? Was she over-gunned or badly ballasted? Or was she badly handled? Up to the present there has been very little to go by. Parts of the record of the proceedings of the inquiry have never been found and a lot of questions still remain unanswered. Soon, however, we shall be able to know whether the doubts thrown on her stability were justified or not. To settle this point, we need a plan of her hull, a working-drawing to enable the weight and point of gravity of the hull to be determined, and, no less important, a plan of the rigging so that we can know what that weighed. Another thing that must be known is the ship's draught at the time of the accident; and, finally, we must have some idea of the weight of the crew and equipment and how the latter was placed about the ship. Equipment includes armament, provisions and ballast. None of this will be easy to do, because no plans were ever made in those days and, if there was a specification, it has not been found. Even if it were, it would probably give fairly scant details, judging by that for a larger ship, dated 1631, that has been preserved. This gives only the length, breadth and height of the keel; the length along the stem; the breadth within its skin; the depth of the hold; the distance between the top deck and upper battery deck; the dimensions of the shell; its rise; the thickness of the planks; and the thickness and breadth of foot-waling used to strengthen and protect the ship. That apparently is all that the shipwrights of those days had to go on and it does not seem very much.

Particular thought was given to the shape of the rib at the point of maximum breadth, since that to a certain extent dictates the shape of the whole hull. Otherwise ships were built in accordance with the master-builder's own ideas and the custom of the age, the only limitations being the knowledge and experience of those concerned.

The design of the hull is, of course, of very considerable importance for a ship's stability. Several witnesses at the inquiry stated that *Vasa*'s dimensions were faulty, that her hull was too narrow and her bottom too pointed, and also that there was not enough room in the bilge for the requisite amount of ballast. How much truth there is in this cannot be known till we have the plans of the ship, and these can be studied and perhaps compared with those of contemporary foreign ships that may be preserved, it having been the custom elsewhere in Europe to make plans, even if only simple ones, of ships to be built.

Fortunately, in Denmark, they have found the plans of a ship that can almost certainly be identified as the *Sankta Sofia*, a flagship built between 1624 and 1627 by a Scots shipwright who had settled in Denmark, David Sinklar. Unfortunately the plan of the ribs is missing, but the rest should be enough to make a comparison of the two ships, which are roughly of the same size, possible. It may be of importance here that the *Sankta Sofia* was probably built in the English style and *Vasa* in the Dutch. There may be a certain difference in the shape of the two ships' bottoms, which must be taken into consideration when estimating their dimensions and hydrostatic data. Another detail is that *Sankta Sofia*

117

carried only fifty-four guns on two decks, while *Vasa* had sixty-four on three decks. But the main dimensions would appear to have been pretty similar, and we know that the Danish ship was 'stiff' or stable, because she remained in service until 1645, when she was lost in a storm off Gothenburg, to be found again in 1961.

The most important and the most difficult part of the problem of *Vasa*'s stability is the question of determining where her centre of gravity originally lay. The old sources give no information about this and the work of determining it will have to be based on a number of more or less conjectural assumptions, but once the hull and its high sterncastle have been reconstructed, it should be possible to arrive at this more or less accurately.

The ballast has all been taken out now and weighed, and we know too how it was stowed. The total weight of the ship's armament is known as well and also, generally speaking, how the guns were distributed on the three decks. We know where the ammunition was stowed. It is considerably more difficult to establish where the provisions and other equipment were kept and how much it all weighed. A more or less greater quantity of equipment must have been lost overboard when the ship capsized and the seventeenth-century divers may also have salvaged a certain amount. All that makes calculation no easier.

A big item of weight is the rigging. We have no contemporary information about this or the size of the sails, etc.; but fortunately the lower parts of both the mainmast and foremast have been salvaged and, on the basis of the information they provide and what we know of other contemporary ships, it should be possible to arrive at a pretty accurate picture of how *Vasa* was rigged and so determine the weight of her rigging. We know what sail she was carrying when she went down, and so the centre of gravity of the sails can be determined. Also we know the direction of the wind and can estimate *Vasa*'s approximate course.

At the inquiry various witnesses gave evidence about *Vasa*'s draught at the time. This does not entirely agree, but when we arrive at an estimate of *Vasa*'s weight, it will probably indicate which figure should be taken as correct.

Another point that may prove of significance is that of the stability-test carried out by Admiral Klas Flemming. Although the result seems to have been pretty discouraging, the admiral seems to have allowed *Vasa* to sail without taking any further measures. What we know about this may, in conjunction with other data, provide extra facts that will complement our rather fragmentary knowledge.

The hydrostatic calculations and those to determine *Vasa*'s stability will be worked out on a machine, EDB, put at the *Vasa* Committee's disposal by AB Facit. It is rather nice to think that this most modern of equipment is being used to solve a problem that should have been resolved 334 years ago.

Index

VASA, THE KING'S SHIP

Franzen, Anders, 1, 2-3, 6, 9-11, 93
Frigg (pontoon), 64, 70, 75, 87, 88, 89
Frogmen, 4, 86, 95
Funeral ships, 52

Galley, ship's, 110
Gamla Svardet, 40
Gert (wood-carver), 78
Gierdsson, Lieutenant Petter, 22-3
Glass-sickness, 115
Gokstad ships, 52
Göta Lejon (cruiser), 61
Gothenburg, 42, 43, 46, 118
Green Hunter (*Gröne Jägaren*), 8
Gun-carriages, 109
Gun-ports, 21, 22, 23, 24, 27, 29, 56-7, 79, 84, 103
Guns, 7, 8, 16, 21, 23, 28, 45, 49, 55, 79-81, 83, 117-18
Gustaf Adolf VI, 104-5
Gustav V dock, Stockholm, 2, 10, 11, 88
Gustavus I (*Vasa*), King, 8, 17
Gustavus Adolphus II, King, 9, 14, 26, 27-8, 35, 40, 104, 108
Gyllenhielm, Admiral Carl Carlsson (Court of Inquiry president), 21, 22, 33-4

Hafström, Captain-Commander Georg, 21
Halland, H.R.H. the Prince of, 83
Hans, Master (wood-carver), 78
Hansson, Söfring (*Vasa*'s captain), 15, 16, 19, 20, 24, 26-7, 33, 40, 96
Hedberg, Captain, 64, 71, 87-8, 91, 101, 105

Historians, International Congress of (1960), 46, 84-5
Hybertsson, Master Henrik (shipbuilder), 26, 34, 36

Independence, War of (1523), 8
International Congress of Historians (1960), 46, 84-5
Isbrandsson, Johan, 28-9

Jacob church, Stockholm, 78
Jacobsson, Hein (builder of *Vasa*), 20, 25-8, 34
Johan (wood-carver), 78
John II, Casimir of Poland, 6
John III, King of Sweden, 7
Jonsson, Erik (master of ordnance), 16, 19, 21-2
Jonsson, Captain Hans, 16, 19

Kastellholm, 17, 92
Key of the Realm (*Riksnyckeln*), 7, 9, 80
Kronan (man-of-war), 29

Landskrona, 43
Landsort island, 6
Ledens, Marcus (wood-carver), 78
Liberton (salvage expert), 49
Lodbrok (floating-crane), 92, 93, 100
Lübeck Eagle (*Lybska Ornen*), 7-8
Lustholmen, Stockholm, 17
Lybska Ornen (*Lübeck Eagle*), 7-8
Lybska Svan (*Swan of Lübeck*), 8

Mälaren, Lake, 2
Mansson, Henrik, 40
Maritime History, Museum of, 3, 58

122